# Finding Me

# Finding Me

## A Decade of Darkness,
## a Life Reclaimed

*a memoir of the Cleveland kidnappings*

## Michelle Knight

WITH MICHELLE BURFORD

WEINSTEIN
BOOKS

Copyright © 2014, 2015 by Lillian Rose Lee

Printed in the United States of America

Editorial production by Marrathon Production Services. www.marrathon.net

Book design by Jane Raese
Set in 12-point ITC New Baskerville

Library of Congress Cataloging-in-Publication Data is available for this book.

ISBN 978-1-60286-279-1 (U.S. paperback edition)
ISBN 978-1-60286-256-2 (U.S. hardcover edition)
ISBN 978-1-60286-257-9 (U.S. e-book edition)
ISBN 978-1-60286-295-1 (U.K. paperback edition)
ISBN 978-1-60286-264-7 (U.K. hardcover edition)
ISBN 978-1-60286-265-4 (U.K. e-book edition)
ISBN 978-1-60286-266-1 (International paperback edition)
ISBN 978-1-60286-267-8 (International e-book edition)

Published by Weinstein Books
A member of the Perseus Books Group
www.weinsteinbooks.com

Weinstein Books are available at special discounts for bulk purchases in the U.S. by corporations, institutions, and other organizations. For more information, please contact the Special Markets Department at the Perseus Books Group, 2300 Chestnut Street, Suite 200, Philadelphia, PA 19103, call (800) 810-4145, ext. 5000, or e-mail special.markets@perseusbooks.com.

FIRST PAPERBACK EDITION

10 9 8 7 6 5 4

For Joey

# Contents

# CONTENTS

# Preface

THE DAY I DISAPPEARED in 2002, not many people even seemed to notice. I was twenty-one—a young mom who stopped at a Family Dollar store one afternoon to ask for directions. For the next eleven years I was locked away in hell. That's the part of my story you may already know. There's a whole lot more that you don't.

I've never talked about the painful life I had even before I was kidnapped. I've never revealed why I spoke to the man who came up to me in the store or the creepy feeling I had when we left. I've never discussed what really happened between me, Gina, and Amanda inside those walls. Matter of fact, I've never told my whole story. Until now.

I'm not the first person to go through an ordeal like this. And every time a big kidnapping case comes up everyone is shocked: Jaycee Dugard, who spent eighteen years chained up in a backyard shack in California; Elizabeth Smart, who was taken from her bedroom in Salt Lake City the same summer I was abducted; Shawn Hornbeck, the Missouri boy who was snatched while riding his bike to his friend's home; and in November 2013 the three London women who were found after spending thirty years in slavery. These kinds of stories are big news, but when they fade away, it's easy to forget all the people who are still missing. That's one reason

I'm opening up my life in this book: I want everyone to re-member those who are lost.

And I want to urge you that if you ever notice anything that seems off about a situation—a child who keeps missing school, a woman who doesn't seem able to leave a house—please do call the police and ask them to check it out. Don't worry about seeming foolish if it turns out to be fine. At least you'll have the peace of mind that comes from knowing that you could have helped someone who was in trouble. Please, always take the two minutes to make that call.

INVISIBLE—THAT'S HOW I felt for the nearly four thousand days I survived in Ariel Castro's hellhole. Every single day all I could think about was getting back to my son, Joey. I wouldn't have believed this before it happened to me, but I now know that anyone can be kidnapped. Anywhere. Any-time. And on the summer day when it happened to me, not too many people seemed to care. Nobody had a vigil. It wasn't all over the news. Neither my relatives nor the neigh-bors got together and put up flyers. The whole world moved on as if I was never even alive. I felt like I was screaming at the top of my lungs, but no one could hear me.

Every person who is lost is somebody's child. We will never know all their names, but we can still keep them in our thoughts. As I mentioned, we can also speak up when something seems fishy. My eleven years would have been a lot shorter if more people had paid attention and then actu-ally taken a moment to call the cops.

As hard as it has been to look back on what happened to me, it was even harder to live through it. Some of my memories are all over the place. I don't even know if it's possible to make sense out of chaos, but that's what I've tried to do. I have probably left out some things, but this is what I recall after being held captive for eleven years. The man who took away a huge part of my life would have wanted me to stay quiet. But that's exactly why I shouldn't. Even before I found myself in the wrong place at the wrong time, I felt like I didn't have a voice. So now I want to speak up for all those missing women and children who still aren't being heard. I hope there will never be another person who feels like I did for so many years: Thrown away. Ignored. Forgotten.

Yes, I made it through one of the most terrible experiences that can happen to a human being, but most of all, my story is about hope. I might have been chained, starved, and beaten, yet that monster couldn't totally crush my spirit. Over and over I chose to get back up and keep going. Now I'm going to tell you how I did it.

# Finding Me

# 1

## Found & Lost

I woke up early that morning in September 2013 around 5 A.M. The night before, I could barely even sleep. A whirlwind of thoughts went through my head. *What has Joey's life been like since I last saw him? What does he look like, now that he's fourteen? Is he happy in his new home? Is he doing well in school? What does he want to be when he grows up? Does he even know that I'm his mom?*

There were so many questions I wanted to ask, so many years I had missed. I really wanted to see my son in person, but I couldn't—at least not yet. The family who adopted him when he was four was concerned about interrupting his life. I completely understood that, but it still broke my heart.

"For now," my lawyer Peggy had told me, "they are willing to send some photos of him. But you have to keep them private to protect his identity." On the morning of our meeting we were getting together so she could show them to me.

Peggy handed me the pages, and I spread them out on the table. There were eight photocopied pictures, four on each page. As soon as I saw the first one, hot tears ran down my face.

"Oh my God, he looks just like me!" I said. Joey had on a blue baseball jersey and wore a cap down over his dark, curly hair. He stood with his bat over his arm. The photo seemed current. He still had that cute button nose, and he looked tall for his age—he must've gotten his height from his father, who was six foot. But that big smile, those small ears, and those big, juicy lips? Those things came straight from me. I moved the pictures to the side so the water dripping from my cheeks wouldn't ruin them. Peggy handed me a tissue.

"Look," I said through my tears, "he loves baseball the same way I do!"

One at a time, I stared at every picture. In the second photo he looked about seven and was kneeling and wearing a suit. In the next he was mixing some cookie dough in a bowl. "He likes to cook, like me!" I exclaimed. Besides the baseball picture, there was one where he was holding a hockey stick, another where he was wearing a scuba outfit in a pool, and one where he was rollerblading.

"Wow, he must really be into sports," I said.

Peggy nodded and smiled at me. In every single photo he looked happy. Very happy.

Slowly I ran my fingers across Joey's face. I wanted to touch him and hug him. Tell him how much I had missed him. But five months after I escaped from my prison with the hope of finding Joey again, this was the closest I could come to him.

When I got home that night, I pulled out the pictures and stared at them again. As I looked at Joey's bright eyes and big smile, I felt every single emotion a mother who has lost a child can feel. Like regret. Things could have been so different for us. And anger. Why did that bastard have to choose me to kidnap? And also joy and relief. Thank God someone has been taking care of my baby. I tucked the two sheets away in a blue folder, one that I'd already put a butterfly sticker on.

That day in Peggy's office wasn't an ending. In a way, it's where my story begins. I set out searching for my son twice—first when he was only two and a half, and next after we'd been separated for twelve long years. I only hoped that soon I'd be able to give him a big hug once again.

# 2

# My Family

I WILL ALWAYS remember the inside of that brown station wagon—the grimy floor mats and the stink of rotten apples. When I was four that car was where my family lived. Me, my twin two-year-old brothers, Eddie and Freddie, and my little cousin, Mikey, all huddled together in the back of that wagon and tried to stay warm under one small, dirty blanket.

"Scoot over!" Freddie would yell. He was the more talkative of the twins—and the one who usually hogged the covers. He'd curl up his little fist and give Eddie a push. Eddie, who was pretty calm for his age, didn't really push back. Even though they were identical and had the same olive skin and dark, curly hair, I could usually tell them apart by who was doing the most shoving.

"Stop pushing him, Freddie," I'd say. Because I was about two years older, that made me the big sister in charge of settling the arguments. "Here, you guys can have some of my covers," I'd tell them when they'd all start jerking the blanket back and forth. "Just stop fighting." That would work for about three minutes before they started in again. I loved all of them, even if they did drive me crazy.

On some days my dad parked next to an apple orchard on the outside of Cleveland. We picked our meals right off the tree. I ate green apples until my stomach hurt. "Put these extras in the back so we can have them later on," Ma would say. She tossed one apple at a time from the front seat back to us. After I caught one, I used it to play hide and seek with little Mikey, who had brown hair and was very skinny.

"Guess where I hid mine?" I'd ask. Mikey would just shrug and grin.

"I know, I know!" yelled Freddie. "It's behind you!"

I pulled it out from behind my back, waved it in Mikey's face, and he cracked up. He fell for that trick every single time. For hours we entertained ourselves with silly games like that. And every time we drove over to the orchard, we hid so many of those apples in back that we sometimes forgot where we put them. That's why the whole car stank.

I don't know how we ended up homeless—or how we got to Ohio in the first place. My parents never talked much about their lives. Over the years I did pick up on a few things. Like one time Ma told me she was mixed with Irish, black, Hispanic, Indian, Arabic, and Italian. "We're mutts," she said. That must be where my big lips came from, especially because she had them too. And sometimes I heard her saying words in Spanish or Arabic, so at least that part must have been true. She also liked to say, "Children should be seen and not heard."

I had lots of questions: Did she grow up speaking those languages? Did her parents teach them to her? Had she always lived in Ohio? But the adults I knew didn't tell any of us kids what was going on. As my dad would say if I asked a question about his life: "That's grown folks' business." That's why I have no clue where or how they grew up.

I think we spent maybe a whole year in that station wagon. Once we did move, our life wasn't much better. I don't know what that first neighborhood was called, but I do know our three-bedroom house was in the ghetto. There were prostitutes, pimps, and drug dealers standing on the corners. There were drive-bys. And down the street there was a liquor store that stayed open all night long. We were only in that house for a hot minute. All throughout my childhood we moved so many times, it wasn't even funny. I think we must have gone to a new house every two or three months. Seriously. My aunt and cousin moved along with us. A lot more family members came later, but I'll get to that in a minute.

No matter where we moved, it was always in one of the worst parts of town. Cleveland has two sides, east and west, and the Cuyahoga River runs right through it. We mainly stayed on the west side. The couple of times we drove to the other side of the river, I noticed that people over there lived in huge houses with big, green front yards. The streets looked so clean, like you could eat right off of them. The air even smelled better. I wished we could have lived in that part of town. I didn't want to go back home; it was a dump. Whenever I saw something on TV about the projects in another city, I would say to myself, "That looks better than our neighborhood." To be honest, it was a real pit.

I do remember one area we moved around in a lot— Tremont. It's near downtown. In the parts we stayed in there were a lot of gangs and drugs. The sidewalks were littered with needles. At least once a week I heard a gun go off in the middle of the night. *Boom!* Eddie, Freddie, Mikey, and I all shared a room back then, and we'd go hide in the corner of the tiny closet.

"Are you okay?" I asked Eddie. His lips were shaking.

"Yes," he whispered. I could tell he was just as scared as I was. But being the protective older sister, I faked it and acted strong. "It's going to be okay," I always told him.

I thought the inside of our first house was gross. It had an upstairs and a downstairs, and there were four bedrooms. The carpet was brown, with some nasty stains on it. Our bathroom was nasty too, and the stove was broken.

After we moved into that house, a whole bunch of relatives came to stay with us. I kept thinking, *Where were all these people while we were living in that station wagon?* And aside from all the aunts, uncles, and cousins who came to stay with us, I met even more relatives when I got a lot older, like my cousins Lisa and Deanna. Every time a new person moved in I asked, "Who's *that?*" No one ever answered me.

At one point twelve people lived in that one house, so things were very hectic. Plus, total strangers always seemed to be coming and going at all hours of the day and night. The doorbell rang a lot, and scary men often dropped off packages. A lot of nights it was hard to sleep because of the loud parties the grownups were having. Most of the time the whole house reeked.

I didn't have a bedroom that was just mine. My cousins and I were always being switched to different rooms.

"Where are you sleeping tonight?" one of my aunts once asked me.

"I don't know," I told her. "I'll just find a spot."

That night I took my little blue blankct into the room where Eddie and Freddie were and went to sleep right next to their mattress on the floor. Sometimes I slept in my parents' room. Sometimes I even slept downstairs on the living room couch. My brothers and Mikey moved around some too, but they usually stayed in one particular room. For some reason I was the kid who got moved the most, especially if someone new came into the house. It was chaotic, to say the least.

When I was still very young, something happened that changed me forever. In the middle of the night, thirsty, I got up from the twin bed where I was sleeping. I stumbled over a pile of stuff in the dark. When I got to the living room, my mother was sleeping there with her clothes on. I went into the kitchen, put a chair next to the sink, and got some water. When I came back to my bed, a man from my family was sitting right there.

"Don't try to get away," he said in my ear.

I started to cry. My mind went crazy: *Why is he on my bed? Can Ma hear this?*

"Just do what I tell you to, and you won't get hurt," he said. He put one hand into his boxers—and then he put his other hand on my head and pushed me down in front of him. I wanted to scream, but when I tried to, no sounds came out. "If you tell anyone about this," he said, "I will kill you."

I was so scared. All I could do was try to hold back the noise from my crying. Afterward I lay there feeling dirty and all alone.

I never told Ma. I kept thinking about what the man said about killing me. And it didn't happen just that one night. From then on he started messing with me in all different kinds of ways. At first it was a couple of times a week. But as I got a little older, it was almost every day. No matter what bed I wound up in, it seemed like he would sneak in and come find me. I was so frightened, it got to the point where I didn't even want to go to bed at night. Sometimes I would try to stay up really late and hide in a closet. If he couldn't find me, then maybe he would forget to do those nasty things to me. That is what I always hoped, but usually it didn't work.

Mornings were nuts in our house. Sometimes we were able to brush our teeth. Other times, not really. When we could, we did, and that was probably about twice a week. The inside of my mouth always felt grimy and sticky.

"Come over here, Eddie," I would say to my brother, trying to stick a brush in his mouth. While I worked on his teeth, Freddie, Mikey, and about six of my younger cousins would be running all over the place and playing around. We often ran out of stuff like soap and toothpaste, so even after I finished with Eddie, there usually wasn't enough left in the tube for everyone else.

After I got one of the kids' teeth cleaned, I started helping Mikey, who couldn't give himself a bath. "Thank you, Me-Shell!" he would say with a huge grin after I'd washed his hair, dried off his skinny body, and taken him out of the bath tub. He had a hard time pronouncing certain words, including my name. But he was always the sweetest kid.

If there was food in the house, we ate breakfast. My brothers usually had a bowl of Fruity Pebbles. It was the generic kind, but they loved it.

"Fruity Pebbles! Fruity Pebbles! Fruity Pebbles!" The twins would sometimes chant together in the mornings while they ran around upstairs in their Superman under-wear. Fruity Pebbles were one of the only foods they would eat. I couldn't believe they had the nerve to be picky when we barely had enough. Even back then I thought that was weird. I wished my parents had more money to buy us the basics, but it seemed to me that neither of them were able to keep a job for long. Ma did once have a steady job as a nurse, but it didn't last. I'm not too sure what my father or the other adults in the house did. All I knew is that there wasn't enough cash to go around.

For breakfast I usually had a Pop-Tart. I didn't care that much what I ate—I just wanted *something* to put in my stomach to stop it from growling. We rarely had hot food. When our stove was broken, I tried to heat up some ravioli from a can by putting it up against the radiator. That didn't work, but I gave it a shot because I wanted my little brothers and cousins to have something warm for a change. One time I did manage to heat up some hot dogs on that radiator.

"Come over here, you guys," I said, trying to round up all the little ones. "Sit down here on the floor and eat." I lined them up across the dirty carpet and handed out the not-too-hot dogs one at a time. We didn't even have buns. Hot dogs, ramen noodles, cereal, SpaghettiOs, and ravioli—those were the things we always ate. Most of it came out of a can or box.

Before school I always helped my brothers get their clothes on. Freddie was usually bouncing around the room, singing. Eddie, who often copied Freddie, sometimes joined in. Although they looked exactly alike, they didn't have matching outfits. It was all I could do to get a complete set of clothes

on each of them, much less something that matched. Whenever I came into the room they most often slept in, their
clothes were all over the place! Underwear, socks, shirts—
they just threw everything right on the ground. I was always
cleaning up after them.

Once I got them dressed and picked up some of their
stuff, they left for school, which was different from the one
I went to. Then I would brush my shoulder-length brown
hair, squinting at myself through my Coke-bottle glasses (I'd
always had bad eyesight ever since I could remember), and
went to catch my own bus.

Half the time I was barely even in school. It seemed like I
missed at least one or two days a week. The first school I can
remember is Mary Bethune—I think I was in second or third
grade. My mother often came to the school to take me out.
It was either a doctor's appointment, a dentist appointment,
or some other kind of appointment: a death in the family or
someone was getting married. Then I had to make up the
work, and there was tons of it. I hated falling behind like
that. For some reason I felt like I was taken out of school way
more often than my brothers were. But all I wanted was to be
in my class—and to be normal, like the other kids.

When I did go to school, I felt like an idiot. I'd ask the
other kids, "Can you give me the homework assignment
from last week?" If anyone gave it to me, I wrote it down, and
then I did my best to do the work at home. The main reason I hated doing homework was because I missed so many
classes. That's how I ended up flunking out of some grades.
By the time I was twelve and going on thirteen, I had barely
made it through the fifth grade! I was always the oldest kid
in the class, and it stunk.

A few of my teachers did seem worried about how badly I was doing. A couple of them tried to keep me after school so they could help me catch up. But that's hard to do if you're only in class two or three days a week. Why even bother if you're just going to get behind again?

One year a teacher who knew I was failing asked me, "Is everything okay at home?" I paused for a second, but then said yes. As nice as she was, I knew I couldn't tell her the truth about what I was going through.

Nobody was my friend. And I do mean *nobody*. When I was in fourth grade, I went up to a girl in the cafeteria and tried to introduce myself. I said, "Hi, I'm Michelle." I stuck out my hand so she could shake it, but she backed away from me really fast.

"Ooooh, your breath stinks!" she yelled.

I felt completely humiliated. That stopped me from wanting to talk to the other kids, so I hid in the back of all my classes. When the teacher asked me something, I didn't want to talk. One time she said, "Michelle, what's the capital of Ohio?" I knew the answer, but I didn't want to say it out loud because I had trouble pronouncing certain words.

"Colum … um, I mean Columbus," I tried to say. Everybody laughed at me. I wanted to shout, "I'm not retarded!" But I don't think it would have made a difference because people already thought I was slow.

That teacher did try to make everyone be nicer to me. "Class, it's not nice to laugh at another person," she said.

I could tell she felt sorry for me. She and a few other teachers tried to get the other kids to be my friends.

"Why don't you sit with Michelle and share her book?" my reading teacher once told a girl in my class.

"Yuck, she smells funny!" the girl said.

The teacher scolded her and made her come and sit with me anyway, but whenever the teacher turned her back, she pinched her nose. The other kids giggled, and I felt like falling through the floor.

And there were plenty of times when the other kids could make fun of me when the teachers weren't around. In the hallway they yelled "You're so dumb!" and "Stink-ass!" A boy in my math class once said, "You're an ugly retard." I didn't look at him. "The only way a guy would ever love you is if he put a bag over your head," he added.

I acted like it didn't hurt me. But it did. I hated the way I looked, with my unwashed hair and secondhand clothes. I smelled funky. And I was doing horribly in almost every class—mainly D's and F's.

Compared to mine, the other kids' lives seemed much better. For one thing, they had name-brand clothes. Some of them were poor too, but my family looked even worse off.

Many of the grown-ups in my neighborhood were on welfare, but some of them went to work. I often saw groups of women dressed like nurses and maids standing at the bus stop. My parents didn't let us go over to other kids' houses, so I don't know for sure whose mama did what. I do think a lot of folks in the area sold drugs, but at least their kids got enough to eat and some decent clothes out of it! I had maybe two or three outfits. And let me tell you, they weren't brands you would recognize. I wore 1960s shirts that came from Goodwill.

A couple of times some kids at school were actually nice to me. One girl tried to give me some money, but I turned it down. "Thank you," I said, "but that's okay." I didn't think it was right to take her money. And it's not like she really wanted to be my friend—she just felt sorry for me. Because when I tried to say hi to her after that, she turned her back.

There was another girl who also didn't have a lot of money. She always came to school smelling foul. We were on the same level; she didn't talk to anyone because the other kids wouldn't come close to her. One day I brought her some deodorant from my house. I said, "Here, go clean yourself up a little." She took it and told me thank you.

Art was the only class I did like. The teacher was the only one who seemed interested in me. "You have a gift," she told me when she saw one of my drawings. In class I drew all the things I dreamed about. I drew big houses that I wished I could live in. I drew families sitting around the table having dinner. I drew kids in the park with their parents under a blue sky. I drew beautiful butterflies. I drew anything that could take my mind off all the stuff that was happening at home.

For some reason I also loved drawing wolves. I think they're the most beautiful animals I've ever seen. In fourth grade I drew a bunch of wolves on every page of one of my spiral notebooks. At home, even though I was always moving around to different rooms, I kept my notebooks and pencils with me. That was the one and only thing that was just mine.

I also loved music. At a school assembly all the kids stood up and sang the Black National Anthem. "Lift every voice and sing till earth and heaven ring, ring with the harmonies of liberty. Let our rejoicing rise high as the listening skies, let it resound loud as the rolling sea." That song gave me the chills! It still does. Sometimes at night when the man in my house was on top of me, I sang that tune in my head to try to distract myself from what was happening to me.

At home I listened to a ton of radio, mainly R&B. I loved Mariah Carey, Jay-Z, Nas. I loved the beat. Sometimes I would sit in a corner and draw while my cousins slept in another room. If nobody was around, I got up off the floor and danced. Aside from drawing, dancing was one thing I was good at.

Even though I did badly in school, I liked to read and write. My favorite books were horror stories. I read Stephen King novels all the time. And no, they didn't scare me—I loved the thrills and chills. Even now I still take in a lot of horror books and flicks. When I was in fifth grade, I once spent from six o'clock in the evening until early in the morning writing a report about a book I'd liked. I was so proud of what I wrote, and at least that one time I actually got my homework done.

When I stayed home from school, I had to take care of my cousins. Although my parents were at home, they still put me in charge. A lot of my cousins were much younger, and I always had to take care of everybody. There were a ton of cousins in the house: Danielle, Christopher, April, Ricky, Eugena, plus a bunch more.

At one point two babies, who my father nicknamed Kiki and Rah Rah, showed up at our house. They were one and three and had caramel-colored skin and curly afros. I think they were the daughter and son of a family member who wasn't able to take care of them. No one ever told me what happened, but I did take care of those two little kids *a lot.*

Every day I combed Kiki's black curly hair into pigtails and braided Rah Rah's hair in cornrows.

"Ba-ba! Ba-ba! Ba-ba!" Kiki would call out when she wanted me to fill her bottle with milk. While Rah Rah played with a toy truck on the floor, I put Kiki right up in my lap and let her suck down that bottle. They were both so cute, even if they did always need me to change their stinky diapers.

I had some good times with my brothers and cousins. Once, we pulled a prank on Ma on Mother's Day. We all went outside and got this big rock. We put some string on it to make it look like a rat with fur. I put it right on her pillow. When she woke up, she said, "Who put this thing here?" We all fell on the floor laughing! None of us ever confessed who did it, but I'm pretty sure she figured it out.

Eddie, Freddie, and I watched TV together sometimes. We loved a show called *Kenan & Kel*. Kel was this teenage dude, and he would say, "Who loves orange soda? Kel loves orange soda! Is it true? Oh yes, oh yes, it's true-ooo! I do, I do, I do-ooo!" Every time we heard that, we laughed our heads off.

Out of all my cousins, I got along best with April, who was three or four years older than me. For some reason we just clicked. She had a part-time job, so sometimes she had extra money for clothes. She knew I didn't have much, so she shared some of her outfits with me. Once she even let me wear these cool leopard-print pants. "Here, try these," she said. "They'll look good on you."

She also took me places—my parents let me walk to Arby's with her because it was in our neighborhood. "Get whatever you want," she would tell me, pulling out a few dollars from the back pocket of her jeans. I usually ordered the fries; they were so good, especially with hot sauce slathered on them. April was mad cool—mainly because she got me out of that house.

During the summer when I was eleven April offered to take me skating. "Let's walk down to the rink," she said. It was only about fifteen minutes away by foot. "We both need to get out of this house and have some fun!"

I nodded, getting excited. At first my parents didn't want me to go because they didn't have the money. "I have some extra," April said. "I'll cover you."

I threw on some jean shorts and a white tank top. Once April paid the $5 entrance fee for each of us, I put on my skates—a size two. I tried, but I fell down a half-dozen times, right on my butt.

"You're doing great!" April kept telling me. "Just keep going!"

Toward the end of the night a fat kid fell right on me. "Get up!" April yelled. She tried to stop herself from laughing, but she couldn't help it. When I stumbled to my feet, I started cracking up too. On the way home we laughed some more. It was one of the few times I ever felt like a normal kid, being able to do normal things. I loved April for letting me tag along with her and forget about everything else that was going on in my life.

WHEN I TURNED ELEVEN I got my period. The only thing was, I didn't even know it was my period because I had been bleeding down there since I was five. And by the time I was eleven the bad things that were done to me started getting worse. A lot worse.

It could happen anywhere. Like in the basement. Or in any bed around the house. Right after it was over I would lay there and rock back and forth. Later I would get up and go to the bathroom and just sit there on the toilet, blood flowing down. I don't know what I said to God, but I did say some little prayers. Just in case he really was up there, I thought I'd give him a shot. But if he was, I didn't understand why he didn't stop the man. Most of the time I was so sad and miserable that I got used to feeling that way.

By the time I turned fifteen and we were living in a canary-yellow house in Tremont, I got totally pissed off about my whole situation. I wanted to do something to stop the abuse—*anything*. But I wasn't strong enough to fight the man off because, at the time, I only weighed about seventy-five pounds.

So one night not too long before Thanksgiving I sneaked two sleeping pills into his drinking glass. As he drank his bourbon and watched a porno flick, I faked being asleep. I was hoping like hell he would leave me alone for just one night—and he did. The TV was very loud. Once the movie got finished, the screen went blue. He started going to sleep. That's when I scooted my body all the way down under the sheet and waited. And waited.

By about midnight he was snoring. As quietly as I could, I got out of bed. I went over to a dark corner of the room and took off my gown. I put on my favorite pair of black jeans and my T-shirt with a wolf on the front, the one I'd cut the sleeves out of so my shoulders showed. Right about the time when I was pulling the shirt over my head, he made a noise. I froze and held my breath.

After a few seconds he started snoring again. *That was close,* I thought. I rushed to get on my socks and blue sneakers. Then I tiptoed into the room where Eddie and Freddie were sleeping. I had hidden my purple backpack in their closet earlier that day. I checked to make sure they were really asleep, and then I grabbed the straps on my backpack. It was heavy because I had put every piece of clothing I could find in there, and even a couple of my parents' shirts. I also stuffed a thin fleece blanket on the top. The last thing I put in there was a bunch of pencils I got from art class, a little pencil sharpener, and four spiral notebooks. I didn't have a coat.

I already knew how I was going to get out—I had planned it. I put my backpack on my shoulders and went over to the first-floor bathroom because people were sleeping out in the living room. From the window I could see the backyard. As hard as I could, I tried to pull up the window. *Creak, creak.* At first, it got stuck, but then it came open.

I stood on the toilet seat and looked out. *I can't believe I'm doing this,* I thought. I was so nervous that I was going to fall and bust my leg. *Can anyone hear me?* I held my breath because I didn't want anyone to wake up and grab me. One leg at a time, I slid out the window and jumped onto the grass.

I didn't close the window. I didn't look back over my shoulder at the house. I didn't think about whether anyone had seen me get away. I already felt like my family didn't give a rip. If they tried to find me and bring me home, it seemed to me that it could only be for one reason—to have me run around after all those kids.

In the dark I made my way down our street and turned into an alley. I had no clue where I was going or what I would do next. As a matter of fact, I had no real plan at all. The only thing I knew was that I had to get away from that house. That man. That life. The cold air hit me like a thousand knives. What I was about to walk into would be a heck of a lot colder than that.

# 3

## Under the Bridge

"SWEETIE, WHAT YOU DOIN' out here with no coat on?" As the sun came up, a tall black man stood in the doorway of a Baptist church in downtown Cleveland. From a few feet away on the sidewalk, I stared up at him. He had a triangle-shaped haircut and a thick moustache. He gave me a big smile and waved me toward the door. "You know, you should come on inside," he said. "You can have something to eat with us."

My hands stiff from the cold, I came over to the door. Right inside the church's entrance were some stairs leading down to a dining hall, where twelve or so homeless people were already in line. I took my place at the end of it. That's how my Thanksgiving Day started. *At last,* I thought. *I'm going to get to eat!*

I'd been homeless for one whole week. After I left the house that night I walked for a couple of hours. I wanted to get as far away as I could so I wouldn't run into any of my parents' neighbors or friends. Eventually I made my way over into a small park and found a stack of newspapers someone had left on a bench. I spread them out underneath the bench and got down under there like it was a little bed. I used my backpack as a pillow. I was so sleepy, but when you're homeless, you really can't sleep. You're always afraid that a stranger might come up behind you in the dark to rob you or stab you. I dozed off a couple of times that night. But whenever I heard a car passing or a nasty rat digging through a trash can, my eyes opened quickly.

Once the sun was up, I mostly walked around—like all day long. I kept my head down low and tried not to look at anyone. I didn't want some little old lady to stop me and call the police because she thought I was eight! That's the thing about being short—no matter how old you are, people always think you're a little kid. And at fifteen, I *was* still a kid. I just wasn't one who felt she could go home.

As I walked, I thought about how I could make it on the streets. In order to last out there, I knew I had to get some stuff together. So one day while I was wandering through a neighborhood, I saw a bat that some kid had left in his front yard. Without even thinking, I snatched it. That evening I returned to the park and slept with all ten fingers wrapped around it. This was my new weapon. *If anybody comes after me,* I thought, *I'm gonna take 'em out!*

After three more nights under the bench, I knew I needed to find a warmer place. I was freezing my butt off. To ward off the cold, I put on every piece of clothing in my bag and wrapped that thin fleece blanket around my shoulders. But even after I did, the cold still cut through all those layers. And I was also pretty scared to be sleeping alone in a park— more like *terrified.* So with my bat gripped tightly in my hand, I started roaming the streets to look for a place where I could set myself up. That's how I found the bridge.

Actually, it wasn't really a bridge—it was more like a highway overpass. In fact, I had to scoot down some grass on a steep little hill just to get underneath it. Once I made it down there, I knew right away that it was exactly what I was looking for. Private. No cops. And no other homeless people already down there. Every time a car whipped by on the freeway above, the overpass shook. *Even better,* I thought. I figured the loud sound from the engines would drown out any noise I made.

Later in the afternoon I laid my bag and bat on a short row of bricks beneath the underpass, and I slept. For five hours straight. Yes, it's dangerous for a girl to sleep under a bridge, but it felt a helluva lot safer than sleeping under a park bench! Plus, when you've been in bed with a sicko, you're not used to feeling safe. I hoped the bridge was outside of town, but I did know that it wasn't too far away from where my parents lived. It seemed like my dad had driven us around the area before. I just hoped I was far enough away so they wouldn't find me.

When I awoke that night, I looked everywhere through a nearby neighborhood for something else I could use to protect myself. In the backyard of one house there was a huge blue plastic garbage can with a lid. *Heck, yeah.* There were no lights on in the house, so I took my chances that everybody was gone for a while. I tipped the can to dump it and dragged it across the yard and onto the sidewalk. It was almost as tall as me, so I had a hard time lifting it. I had to be careful not to make noise so I wouldn't wake up the whole neighborhood. Finally I got it all the way back to the grassy hill. I rolled it down the hill and watched it come to a stop, and then I crawled down after it.

Late that night I turned that can into my bedroom. I left it on its side so I could scoot in. Once inside, I spread my fleece over me. Only my feet hung out over the edge. I was a little bit warmer inside the can, but it was still cold. My teeth chattered and my stomach growled. I wondered what was happening to Eddie and Freddie, left behind at the latest house we'd moved to. *Who was taking care of them? Who was making sure Mikey got bathed and fed?*

To distract myself, I pulled out a notebook and pencil from my backpack. Holding the paper up to my face in the pitch dark, I drew one of my favorite things, a butterfly—or at least I thought I did. When I looked at the page the next morning, it didn't look too much like a butterfly. It looked like a two-year-old had scribbled on it.

By the time Thanksgiving rolled around, I was starving. Other than a turkey sandwich I'd ripped off from a grocery store a couple of days before and a few scraps of food I'd found here and there, I hadn't eaten a crumb. To be honest, I'd almost forgotten it was Thanksgiving; when you're homeless, you tend to lose track of time. It's not like you have a calendar, and I didn't own a watch. Anyway, that morning I happened to pass the Baptist church. The delicious smell of cooking coming from the open front door made my mouth water. That's the real reason I stopped.

"What's your name, sweetie?" the tall black man asked after he followed me downstairs to the church's dining hall.

"My name is Michelle." I didn't look him in the eye because I was embarrassed about how funky I smelled. I hadn't bathed since I'd left my house seven days before. My brown shoulder-length hair was matted on one side, and the other side was sticking out all over. My black T-shirt was covered with lint and dandruff. "You know what?" he said. "I might have a coat that fits you. After you eat, why don't you come with me and we'll take a look?"

"Thanks," I said, looking directly at him for a second. For a minute I wondered why he was being so nice to me, but then I realized he was just a friendly church type.

I stuffed my face at the southern-style buffet. The crispy fried chicken was so good, it practically melted on my tongue. I dug into mashed potatoes and gravy, stuffing, and cranberry sauce. I thought I'd died and gone to heaven when I sampled the baked macaroni and cheese, collard greens, and corn. And the biscuits! I must have gobbled up five or six of them. For some weird reason there was no turkey, but I didn't care. I ate so much, I had to unbutton the top button of my jeans. As soon as I devoured the first plate, I went back for a second. Then a third. I didn't want to look greedy, but I didn't know when the next time would be that I could eat again. And everything was delicious; it seemed like the best meal I'd ever had in my life.

As I was cramming in another buttermilk biscuit, the man with the triangle haircut stopped by. "People tell me I look like Arsenio Hall because of my hair," he joked. "Do you think I look like Arsenio?"

I smiled, nodded, and put another bite in my mouth.

"Slow down there, honey," he said. "If you eat any faster, you're gonna hurt yourself!" I kind of laughed with my mouth full of biscuit.

When the dinner was over, Arsenio kept his promise—he went to a bin of used clothing and pulled out a puffy orange coat with a hood. It was at least three sizes too big, and it hung down past my knees. But when he gave it to me, it was like he handed me a check for a million bucks. That's how amazing it was to go back to the bridge with an extra layer. Plus a full stomach. And a little bit of hope that maybe the whole God thing wasn't just a bunch of bull.

That day the church workers sent us off with another gift—a bag of stuff that local charities had donated. There was a comb, a little bottle of shampoo, a toothbrush, and a small tube of toothpaste. Do you know what it's like not to brush your teeth for *days*? The inside of my mouth felt like I'd spread a stick of butter all over it. It was gross. I took the bag of stuff back to my trash can and put it in the back of the bin. I wanted to make sure no one stole my new prizes.

That night at Thanksgiving dinner one of the volunteers had made an announcement that the church gave out a free meal every weekday at around 5 P.M. *Sweet.* That was the main reason I went back the next evening. And the next. And the next. In fact, hardly a day went by that Arsenio and the other members didn't see me hustling down the street trying to make it there in time for dinner (like I said, I didn't have a watch!).

I even started going over there on Sunday mornings. They didn't serve food then, but there was music. And it was just beautiful. I stood in the back as the choir sang "Angel of Mine." I had never heard anything like it. Their voices wrapping around the melody lifted my soul, and for a few minutes I was able to forget about my desperate situation. When those men and women in robes swayed and sang, something warm and happy brimmed up in me. I felt soothed and calm, uplifted even. People in the pews turned to smile at me and at each other. At that moment I felt connected to every single person in that church. *If there* is *a heaven,* I thought, *this must be how the choir there sounds.*

"Come on in here, girl!" a couple of the older women told me one morning when they saw me standing in the back. Their smiles looked so kind, but at first I didn't want to sit next to anyone. After a couple of weeks, though, I began scooting onto the last pew to listen to the service. From there I figured most of the people probably couldn't smell me. After that I started cleaning myself up a bit beforehand in the church's small single bathroom.

How do you take a "bath" in a church restroom? Let me explain. First you lock the door. Then you get a stack of paper towels. Next, if you're as short as I am, you empty the trash can and scoot it over to the sink so you can stand on top of it. From there you turn on the faucet, dip your head under the running water, and rinse it the best way you can. The whole time you pray that no one will knock on that door or shout out to ask why you're taking so long.

You quickly use paper towels to dry your hair and face. Then you wet more towels to wipe down the funkiest places on your body. After that you put the trash can back, snatch up all the paper from the floor, and stuff it into the can. On your way out you grab a bunch of paper towels you can later use to stuff down in your pants during that time of the month. Then you sneak back into the church with your hair still a little wet, hoping that "Angel of Mine" is coming up next.

I could have taken a quick bath in a restroom at a McDonald's, but I didn't want to chance it. I figured that if I did my bathing at a church, I might not get thrown out if someone realized what I was doing. Church people are usually nicer than that. In fact, some of the ladies probably knew I was washing off in there, but they never said anything about it. On most weekends I was able to clean up a little in their bathroom. Plus I got to eat a lot of scrumptious fried chicken and hear the best music I'd ever heard in my life.

MY PLAN TO keep to myself had worked out: no one ever bothered me under that bridge. But all of that changed late one night.

"I see you're in need of money." It must have been a long time after midnight when I heard a man's voice from inside my trash can. My eyelids snapped opened. I grabbed my bat and scooted to the edge of the bin, with just my head sticking out. I was ready to jump up and swing at whoever this was.

A guy was standing there. From what I could make out in the darkness, he looked like a mix of black and Latino. He had on a black leather jacket with some baggy jeans and sneakers, and he was about six feet tall.

"Wait a minute—you don't have to do that," he said when he noticed me clutching the bat. "I'm not gonna hurt you."

I stared up at him.

"How old are you?" he asked.

I don't know why I answered him, but I did. "I'm fifteen," I told him. "Why do you need to know that?"

In the moonlight he had one of the whitest smiles I'd ever seen. "By the way, I'm Sniper," he said. "I might have a job for you, but I needed to know how old you are."

I figured a homeless person was only ever offered two jobs: a gig that came with sex or drugs. "I guess I don't have to ask where you got that name," I told him. "Do you go around beating people up or something?"

He laughed. "You're so funny," he said.

I didn't see what was so funny, especially when a strange guy was standing in my spot. I wasn't sure if I should climb out of the trash can and try to run or stay inside and hope he'd go away. Then again, he didn't give off a violent vibe, so I decided to stay in the can for another minute.

"I sell weed and E," he added. "I'm looking for a runner."

*I don't know if I want to screw around with something like this. It could get scary,* I thought. But I was broke. I was starving and cold as hell. And I felt desperate for some money. Maybe I could just do it long enough to get together some cash for my own place.

"Why don't you come with me and we'll talk about it?" he asked.

I crawled all of the way out of the bin and got up on my feet, staggering a little because my legs were numb from the cramped way I'd slept. I stuffed my things into my backpack, tied the fleece blanket around my waist, and looked at him.

"What's your name?" he asked, eyeballing me up and down the way people do when they're trying to figure out if I'm a dwarf.

"It's Michelle."

"Follow me," he said. I'm not sure why I trusted him; I just had a gut feeling that he wouldn't hurt me. You would think I would've been scared out of my mind, and looking back on it, I should have been. But I was so sick of sleeping in a trash can and never having enough to eat that I was desperate. So I followed him up the grassy hill.

On the other side of the overpass he walked me to where his car was parked. The windows were completely tinted—a definite sign that he really was a drug dealer. He then opened the back door and pointed for me to climb in. I did.

"I'm on my way to do a deal tonight," he said. "I want you to stay real quiet in the backseat, okay?" I nodded. "There's no reason for them to know you're with me. Later on I'll take you to my place." He shut the door, opened the driver's side, and slid behind the steering wheel. In the car's interior light I saw that he was probably around eighteen years old.

We drove for about a half hour before Sniper slowed down to a stop. He got out and started talking to a group of men. I could hear them speaking fast in Spanish, but I couldn't make out a single word. He popped open the trunk and gave one of the men a large package. *Must be weed*, I thought. After about twenty minutes he got back in the car and looked over his shoulder at me.

"You still all right back there?" he asked. I nodded. "Let's get outta here," he said. We drove for a while before we pulled into a driveway.

When we got out of the car, Sniper walked me up his driveway and unlocked the front door. I stopped for a minute. *I still don't know this guy. What will happen inside his house?* But I decided to take a chance. I figured it couldn't be much worse than what I had gone through during the first fifteen years of my life. I took a step inside.

"Welcome home," he said.

I looked around the living room. The place was totally pimped out. He had a waterfall and a fish tank. His walls were bright white, and it smelled like he had just put on a fresh coat of paint.

"Let me take you upstairs to the room where you'll be staying," he said. "I'll sleep on the couch and give you my room." At the top of the stairs he pointed to a door on the right. "Another kid named Roderick stays in my second bedroom," he said. "He's a runner too. I'll introduce you to him later." I didn't know exactly what a drug runner would do, but I could see that I was going to get one thing out of it—a warm place to sleep.

Sniper's room was just as pimped out as the rest of the place. His bed had a zebra-print comforter and white silky sheets. A large ceiling mirror hung over the queen-size mattress; I could guess what he used that for. The bathroom just off the bedroom had a big round tub with a red and black shower curtain.

"Get yourself cleaned up," he said. He handed me a towel, a new bar of soap, and a pair of women's pajamas that he said his little sister had left there. I wondered if he'd had another girl runner at some point and what had happened to her. "Do you need anything else?" he asked.

I could feel my face turning red as I pointed down between my legs. He gave me a weird look. "Oh, I get it," he said. "I'll be right back." A few minutes later I heard him pull out in the car. He returned with a box of tampons and gave them to me; I assumed he'd made a quick run to the twenty-four-hour drugstore.

After he left the room, I stripped off my nasty jeans and that T-shirt with the wolf printed on the front. Then I turned on the shower, stepped into the tub, and stood directly under the head. For about an hour. When you haven't been able to really clean yourself up for weeks, a whole lot of dirt builds up. The hot water that slid off my body and swirled into the drain was totally black for at least the first twenty minutes.

"Are you okay in there?" Sniper yelled from the room.

"I'm fine," I shouted back. "Just filthy."

"All right. I'll be downstairs if you need anything."

Once I pulled on the polka-dotted PJs that were way too long for me, I crawled under his fluffy comforter. The mattress felt unbelievably soft; I hadn't slept in a bed in weeks. *Is this real?* I thought. *Am I really here? Is this guy going to keep treating me this nice, or is he going to turn on me and attack me?* Even though I was nervous, I was so exhausted that I sank down into the mattress and went right to sleep.

The next morning I woke up to the smell of sizzling sausage. Sniper thumped up the stairs and tapped on my door. "Good morning, Michelle," he said. "Come down when you're ready for breakfast." Once I went down to the dining room I saw a boy with dark hair already sitting at the table. His skin was walnut brown, and he was wicked thin. I figured he must be Roderick.

Roderick said something to me, but I had no idea what. His Saudi Arabian accent was so thick that at first it was hard to make out his words.

"He's asking your name," Sniper cut in with a chuckle.

"I'm Michelle," I told the boy. "Nice to meet you." When he responded, I managed to catch what he said. "Hi, Chapo."

"That's what we're going to call you around here— Chapo," Sniper added. "That's Spanish for *little*." I didn't mind. In fact, the nickname stuck.

Over breakfast Roderick filled me in on a little of his story. I had to ask him to repeat himself a few times, but after a while I got used to his accent. He was sixteen. He'd been surviving on the streets since he was thirteen. Back then his mother had kicked him out of her house because he'd refused to return to his family's homeland in Saudi Arabia. He might have said why he didn't want to go back, but if he did, I didn't catch that part. A few months after he'd become homeless, Sniper had come up to him in the same way that he had me. He'd lived with Sniper and worked for him every day since.

That evening the three of us chilled on the big red couch in the living room and watched a movie together—something I'd never done with my actual family. It felt so good to be part of a group, even if I still didn't know what my role in it would be.

"Tomorrow we've gotta get you a handgun and show you how to shoot it," Sniper said as the movie credits rolled. I stared at him. "Now that you're settled in, it's time for you to go out on your first run," he added. Roderick just kept his eyes glued to the TV screen.

Back upstairs in the bedroom, I climbed onto the mattress and pulled the zebra-print comforter up as far as I could. As I lay there staring up at my reflection in the mirrored ceiling, I thought of my spot under the bridge and the trash can I'd left there. I wondered what Eddie, Freddie, and Mikey were doing. I wondered if the choir at the Baptist church would sing my favorite song that Sunday. And, of course, I thought of how it might feel to hold a gun. It scared the hell out of me.

# 4

## On the Run

SNIPER HANDED ME a .22 Glock—the first gun I'd ever held. "You need to learn how to protect yourself," he told me. "I have to make sure you stay safe. I'm going to take you some-place where I can teach you how to use it." I'm not sure if he noticed, but when he said that, I flinched. Big time. *Does he expect me to shoot people?* I wondered anxiously.

That afternoon we got into his car. In the backseat was a bull's-eye he'd made from a piece of cardboard. We drove to a wooded area out in the boonies, a place where no one would hear gunshots. We got out of the car and went through the trees to an open area. Sniper tied the bull's-eye to a tree trunk. He then showed me how to position the gun to hit the mark.

"Hold it like this, with both hands. Make sure you're bal-anced on both feet, and then point it directly toward the bull's-eye." Then all of a sudden, he pulled the trigger. *Pop!*

The sound of the bullet leaving the gun made me almost pee my pants. Sniper didn't hit the center mark, but he came pretty close. He handed me the gun. "Your turn," he said.

I stood in the same spot he had and aimed at the target. *Pow!* After several tries I managed to hit the edge of the cardboard.

"Good. Do it again," Sniper said. He had me practice a few more rounds before we left.

On the way back to his house we went past the area near where my parents lived. *I wonder if they're still there,* I thought. But I wasn't about to find out. Even with the tinted windows, I slid down as low as I could to be double-sure no one would see me. The day before, when he'd asked me why I'd been living on the street, I had told Sniper what I'd endured in that house. He had listened without saying a word. When I finished talking, he just shook his head. "I don't understand how they could've treated a little girl that way," he said. "It wasn't right for them to put you through all that. They're lucky I don't go find them and shoot them right now." Whenever Sniper talked that way, I didn't feel like his runner. I felt more like a little sister—safe and protected.

Sniper came from a halfway decent family—his mother at least worked a steady job, and he told me he'd never been physically abused. He hadn't told his family he was selling drugs, but I'm sure they must've had an idea since he never invited them to his house, and he always had a lot of cash. For some reason Sniper had dropped out of school when he was fifteen. But I could tell he was smart by the smooth way he spoke and carried himself. Besides, I figured he had to have something on the ball to run the kind of hustle he was operating.

"You should've stayed in school," I once told him.

"Why would I do that?" he shot back. "I can make a lot more money doing what I do." I didn't say anything to that.

That night after my shooting lesson, Sniper told me all about what my new job involved. First, I'd go into a building, a nightclub, or an apartment complex, usually in a part of town where there were a lot of drugs. Once there, I had to identify people who might want a particular drug. I'd then return to the car, where Sniper would be waiting with the goods. I'd tell him what kind and amount of drugs had been asked for, and what price the person was willing to pay. If Sniper thought it all sounded good, I'd return with the dope.

"Whatever you do," he warned me, "never, ever give a person the drugs until after they've given you the cash." If any kind of problem came up, he said, I was supposed to get the freak outta there as fast as possible. And if the situation got really ugly? Well, that was why I carried the Glock. He also gave me a beeper.

One week later the evening of my first run arrived. I'd tried to get Roderick to tell me what he'd gone through since he'd been with Sniper. But whenever I brought that up, he suddenly got quiet. I think he felt protective of me and didn't want to scare me. "You'll be fine, Chapo," he said. I hoped he was right.

That Friday night Sniper backed his car into the garage and packed his trunk with different-sized bags of pot. "Wow," I said. "That's a whole lot of weed." From what he'd said, there must have been $50,000 worth of reefer in there. We got in the car and drove to a building about fifteen minutes away. I wore a long-sleeved navy T-shirt, gray sweatpants, and a black jacket big enough to cover the huge square fanny pack I'd put on around my waist. My hands shaking, I put the safety switch on the gun and put it down in the side of my cotton underwear. We pulled into an alley. As I got out of the

car, Sniper gave me a reminder: "No cash means no drugs."
I gulped and nodded.

That night was very dark. Feeling incredibly nervous as
I held the sides of my jacket closed, I found my way to the
courtyard of the apartment building. I looked up and saw a
dozen people sitting out on their stoops. Everyone seemed
to be lighting up; the courtyard was filled with smoke and the
smell of pot. When I spotted a scrubby-looking, middle-aged
white man rolling a joint, I walked over to him. His pupils
were very dilated, and his eyes were red. Forget weed—he
looked more like a crackhead than a pothead.

"Hey," I whispered. "Want some more of that tonight?"
He kept right on rolling and hardly even looked up at me.
Anxiously I licked my bottom lip.

"Hold on there, kid," he finally said. He stood on the
staircase and disappeared through the front door of one of
the apartments. A moment later he came back with a young
blonde woman. She held her head to the side and looked
directly at me. She seemed even more high than he did.

"We'll take a big bag," the man finally said.

"How much can you pay?" I asked.

He paused. "Five hundred dollars," he said.

*Holy crap,* I thought. *Where in the world do these people get that
kind of money?*

I ran back to Sniper's car and told him what they wanted.
"Okay," was all he said. He went to his trunk, dug down past
all the $25 baggies of pot, and pulled out a much larger bag.
He handed it to me, and I stuffed it inside my coat and made
my way back toward the stairs where the couple was waiting.

"I'll take the money first," I told the man. My voice shook
a little.

"Hell, no!" he shouted. Some of the neighbors looked over at us. "Give me the weed, and then you'll get your damn money."

My pulse got faster. I could feel the cold handle of the gun down in my underwear. "I can't do that," I said softly. "First the cash—then the pot. That's the way it goes."

But the man kept asking for the bag, and he got louder and louder. "Just give me the weed!" he shouted. When he stood up and came toward me, I knew there was only one thing I could do: I took off running.

I rounded the corner and jumped back into the car. "They … won't … give me … the money," I said, totally out of breath.

Sniper stared at me. "What do you mean?" he said.

"I tried to get the man's cash first, like you told me to do, but he wanted the weed first."

Sniper paused. "I'll handle it," he said. "I don't want you getting hurt." I described the couple to him in detail so he could easily find them in the courtyard. Sniper got out and took the bag from me, and I stayed behind. When he returned fifteen minutes later, he wasn't holding the bag of weed. He pulled five $100 bills from his coat pocket and showed it to me. "Sometimes you gotta play a little rough," he said. When he'd appeared around the corner, the sight of him had been enough to scare the bejesus out of the couple. So the man handed over the payment. "Come on, let's get outta here," Sniper said, starting the ignition. My heart was still going a hundred miles per hour.

For the next couple of weeks this was how it went with Sniper and Roderick. By night, the three of us did our runs; by day, we functioned like a little family. We played pool, pinball, and cards in Sniper's basement, laughing until our sides ached. I helped Roderick with his accent (like me, he couldn't pronounce certain words), and he snickered every time I called him by the nickname I gave to him—Flower. Because of his culture, Roderick was a virgin. He would always tell me, "I'm going to save myself for the prettiest girl in the world!" He was such a sweet guy.

Roderick and I hung out every day, but there was never a romantic spark between us. He was like a brother to me. In fact, when I told him I was part Arabic, he gave me a special gift. "This is a scarf that my mother left with me," he said. He held up a pretty blue *hijab*, a head covering that traditional Muslim women wear. "In my culture, when a girl starts her period, she is given this scarf. You're my sister now, so I want to give it to you." I ducked my head down so he could drape the scarf over my hair. "Thank you, Flower," I said, and we both blushed a little.

In exchange for our services, Sniper gave Roderick and me a place to live and a portion of his profits. The two of us usually ended up with about $300 in cash every week. We dipped into our stash to pay Sniper when he got groceries or bought us a couple of six-packs. (Sniper never let us have drugs because he insisted that you couldn't run a great drug business if you became a druggie. But we did have our share of liquor!)

I knew the drugs we sold and delivered were making people's lives a big mess. But as much as I hated handing out weed and going to scary places, I didn't hate that as much as I did the terrible fear and loneliness. And depression. And hours spent drawing wolves and blue skies while shivering inside a plastic garbage can. For the first time in my life I actually felt important. Even loved.

A few weeks later Sniper got busted by the cops not too far from his house. Roderick, who had been with him, managed to get away without the cops seeing him.

"We've gotta clear out of here fast!" Roderick told me once he raced back home. In less than fifteen minutes I stuffed everything I could find into my purple backpack. I pulled on my shoes and coat, grabbed a teddy bear that Sniper had bought me, and dashed out the front door without even locking it.

We had nowhere else to go—so I took Roderick back under the bridge with me. Believe it or not, my trash can was still there. "Nice bedroom, Chapo," he said, kicking the side of the bin. "But you know I can't sleep in there with you—you're a girl." In his culture sharing a bed with a girl you weren't married to would be considered disrespectful and even scandalous. Never mind that he'd been wielding guns and selling marijuana for months.

That same day Roderick swiped his own garbage bin. His can had no lid. He placed his bin right next to mine, spread out his own blanket, and climbed inside. Roderick was at least five foot six, so his legs hung out farther over the edge than mine did.

Although we had enough cash between us to split the first month's rent on a small apartment, we wanted to hold on to our money for the time being. "Let's just stay here for awhile until we can figure out what to do," Roderick said. I quickly agreed.

One evening not even two weeks later, I crawled out of my trash can and made my way up the grassy hill. Roderick followed behind me. I wanted to return to the Baptist church and see if they were still serving meals. I also wanted Arsenio to meet Roderick. Just as I was coming out of our hiding place, on the street above I spotted a woman I recognized. She was a friend of my parents, and I was sure she'd gotten a look at my face. *Damn.*

I tried to back up, but Roderick was right behind me, and I didn't want to sock him square in the face with my foot. "Hey, Michelle!" the woman yelled out. "Hey, come back here, girl!"

I panicked. "Go back!" I said softly to Roderick.

But it was too late. After we got our things from the bins so we could get away from the bridge (so stupid … we should have just left everything there!), we ran up the hill and onto one of the nearby streets. Just as we were rounding a corner, my father drove up beside us.

"Get in the car!" he shouted. That woman had called my father on his cell and told him where she saw me—and he'd sped right over.

My father jumped out and dragged me toward the car. He shoved me into the backseat and hit me upside the head. "That'll teach you not to run away again!" he yelled. You can imagine what kind of trouble I was in once we got home.

When Roderick had seen my father drive up, he freaked out and ran down a side street. My father didn't go after him; he was only interested in getting me back home. I never saw Roderick again.

# 5

## Expecting

IN LATE FEBRUARY, after my father dragged me home from under the bridge, my mother re-enrolled me in school. At sixteen, I was still supposed to be in seventh grade—but I took some kind of test, which I miraculously passed, and the teachers moved me up to the ninth. My return to school felt like stepping back into the same nightmare I'd escaped—only this time things were even worse. Why? Because I actually knew what freedom felt like, and I'd been forced back into prison. My classmates were still mean. My grades were still horrible. So I started ditching class. No one wants to sit at the back of a room and feel stupid and humiliated—and that's how I felt.

At home the family member who'd first raped me was still living with us. So were a bunch of other relatives—the number had grown to about fifteen. The night after I got home the abuse started up again. "You thought you could get away from me, you little pussy," the man hissed into my ear that evening. He swirled his slimy tongue around in my ear. I pulled away in disgust, but he held me close.

Every time he climbed on top of me, I just tried to discon-nect. From the abuse. From my life. From myself. I got to the point where I could make myself not even notice that he was on me. I would make my brain go someplace far away, like to a lush island or to a peach-colored sunset. This scene went down at least three times a week for the next two years. I'm surprised I never turned up pregnant.

One afternoon in my sophomore year I was sitting in the lunchroom. Alone. I was about to eat my cheeseburger, which I'd slathered with my favorite hot sauce.

"How you doin'?" I looked up to see a boy I'd sometimes said hello to around the school. For me to speak to anyone was a rarity, but I thought he was kind of handsome.

The boy, who I'll call Erik, was part white and part black, about six feet tall, and he had the cutest button nose. His arms were very muscular. That day he had on jeans and an army-green T-shirt. "You seem a little sad," he said to me. "Is everything okay with you?"

I shot him a look that said, "Seriously?" He pulled up a chair and sat across from me. I had on a dingy button-up shirt from the 1960s, one of the three homely outfits I owned and wore to death. I also had on a pair of Beetlejuice shoes. I *hated* those shoes!

"Whatever happens in your life," he said with a straight face, "God loves you. He'll always be there for you." This guy was weirding me out. I grabbed a fry from my tray and began chewing it. *Maybe he's some kind of religious freak*, I thought. I kept eating my fries until he eventually got up and left.

A few days later I was sitting in the library—alone again. I was rereading one of my favorite Stephen King novels when

Erik walked over to me. I pretended not to notice him and buried my head farther into the paperback.

"So those are the type of books you like to read—slasher books?" he said.

I smiled and barely looked up. Only because I thought he was handsome, I'd asked a couple of classmates about him. I found out he was on the football team and that he was a senior.

"Do you like poems?" He'd noticed the stack of poetry sitting on the table in front of me. I nodded. "Can you read me something you wrote?" I could feel the blood rushing to my face.

"Well," I said, "I guess so." I looked through the stack and pulled out the poem I considered to be the best. The final line said something about wanting to be loved.

"Why do you feel like that?" Erik asked. I shrugged and put the paper back down on top of the stack.

Over the next few weeks Erik and I began cutting classes together. Often. As strange as I thought he was at first, he was the only person at school who was paying any attention to me. When I was around him, I felt pretty. Even though my clothes were horrible, he always told me that I looked nice. Classmates stared at us as we walked through the hallways together. You could see what they were thinking: "What is he doing with *her*?"

One afternoon when Erik and I were out of class together, he pulled me aside toward a set of lockers. Right then he made things official. "I love you, Michelle," he told me.

I stared at him, not believing what I was hearing. Before I could say anything back, he kissed me long and hard. I was

47

seventeen. It was the first time anyone had ever kissed me in a loving way or said those words to me. It was the best feeling in the world.

I gave Erik the phone number at my house because I didn't have a cell phone. But when he called in the evenings, I usually couldn't answer. I was either chasing around the little kids I had to take care of or I was trying to avoid the relative who abused me.

"Why didn't you call me back?" he'd ask the next day. I never had a good answer. One time, when he really started pressing me about it, I finally told him the truth—or at least part of it.

"Erik, there's something you need to know about me," I said. "I come with a lot of baggage."

"What do you mean by 'a lot of baggage'?" he asked.

I cleared my throat. "Well," I said, "my situation at home is horrible."

"You deserve to be loved," he told me. "I wish I could take you home to live with me."

I wished that too. From what Erik had told me, his parents loved him unconditionally. They treated him well. They bought him stylish clothes and made sure he had dinner every night after school. And not once had anyone ever punched him in the face or sexually abused him. On the nights when I was being violated, I sometimes dreamed of what it would feel like to instead have Erik inside of me—to feel adored rather than despised. About a month into our relationship, I found out.

One Friday afternoon Erik and I ditched class together. For the first time we really made out—all the way. Things got hot and heavy pretty quickly, and we ended up actually doing it. It happened that day, plus three more times. It felt so great to be close to someone because you chose to be. I loved Erik. I also loved that I got to be with him because I wanted to—and not because I was forced.

A few weeks later I began feeling nauseous. And exhausted. I decided to take a pregnancy test. I was terrified. *What will I do if I'm pregnant? How could I support a baby?* That night I took the test. When I saw the blue line, it told me what I pretty much already knew: I was pregnant.

I put down the stick, buried my face in my hands, and cried for an hour. What was I going to do now? I wanted to tell Erik I was pregnant, but that wasn't so simple. Not long after the fourth time we got together a girl had said to me, "You know Erik has a girlfriend, right?"

For a minute I couldn't speak. "You don't know what you're talking about!" I finally blurted out. "That can't be true."

But it was. A girl I'll call Cassie, who went to another high school, rang me up at my parents' house—she caught me on one of the rare occasions when I could come to the phone.

"Hello?"

"This is Cassie," said a high-pitched voice. "I found your number in Erik's phone."

"Who's this?" I asked.

"I don't know if you know this," she began, "but Erik and I have been going out for a few months." I went mute, and she hung up.

For an hour afterward I sobbed. Suddenly I understood what the word *heartache* meant. I felt like someone had pierced my heart with a thousand stickpins.

I began avoiding Erik at school. When our eyes met across a classroom or in the lunchroom, the expression on his face said it all: he knew his girlfriend had told me his secret. A couple of classmates told me that after Cassie had busted him, he began downplaying our relationship. One girl even told me that Erik said, "Michelle was never my girlfriend. She's just someone I fooled around with a couple of times." I never asked Erik about it, but I could tell by the way he was treating me that it might be true. I couldn't believe I'd fallen for his sweet talk, but that was how badly I'd wanted to be loved.

A couple of weeks after Cassie's revelation, I finally ended things with Erik. It wasn't a long conversation, but instead a quick, "I think we both know this is finished." I wanted to get it over with as quickly as possible, like the sudden rip of a Band-Aid from skin that's already sore. I didn't tell Erik I was expecting a baby; I didn't think he deserved to know because of the way he was acting toward me. But I did have to break the news to my mother. A few weeks later I worked up the nerve to tell her. I knew she wasn't happy and that she probably didn't want me to have this baby. But I told her it was my choice, not hers.

As scared as I was, I never even thought about having an abortion. I hoped that at least the baby would love me. At the time I felt like no one else in the world did.

# 6

## Huggy Bear

As I became more exhausted from my pregnancy, I could barely get myself out of bed. And it was embarrassing to attend classes when my stomach started showing. So toward the end of tenth grade I dropped out of school. I'm sure my classmates hardly noticed I was gone.

About five months into my pregnancy my parents split up and my father moved out of the house. I don't know why they parted, but they'd been arguing nonstop for at least a year. After he left, things were a little more peaceful.

Once I dropped out of school, I sat around the house all day and watched TV or read Stephen King books. Thankfully, because I was about as sick as I was huge, my mother cut me a little bit of slack in terms of household responsibilities. By that time the relative who'd been abusing me had backed off some. After so many years, I got pissed off enough that I was determined to defend myself.

"Stop it!" I'd spit when he tried to force himself on me. As petite as I was, I could kick and shove pretty hard—and now when I fought him off, sometimes it worked.

I was excited about the baby coming, and I got even more excited when a nurse told me, "You're having a son." But I was also very scared. As a whole bunch of soap operas, followed by *Judge Judy*, blared on the television during my afternoons at home, my thoughts raced. *What will I do to get money? How will I provide for him? Will I be able to get my own place? Who will hire me without a high school diploma? And if I get a job, will anyone watch the baby for me?* I didn't have any of the answers, but I did know I was supposed to have this child. The way I saw it, the baby growing in my stomach was God's gift to me.

After being abused for so many years, I was still on the fence about God. Did he exist? Did he not? I wasn't 100 percent sure. But if he did exist and was good enough to give me a child to adore, then I decided that might be enough to make up for the hard stuff I went through during my first eighteen years. Each night before I went to sleep I rubbed my belly while singing a little song I'd once heard at that Baptist church: "Now I lay me down to sleep, I pray the Lord my soul to keep," I'd recite. "If I should die before I wake, I pray the Lord my soul to take." It was a simple prayer, a beautiful melody. A call to a God I hoped was real.

A few weeks before my due date I started thinking of names. I picked out one that I really liked—Juliano. But when I mentioned the name to my family, they didn't like it. "Don't give him an ethnic-sounding name," one relative told me. That's how I ended up going with another name I liked just as much—Joseph. For short, I'd call him Joey.

My son came early—by an entire month. I was sitting in the bathtub one evening when my water broke. My mother rushed me to the hospital. The labor was long; as hard as I kept pushing, the child just didn't seem to want to come out. But finally I heard his cries. A nurse cleaned him up, wrapped him in a white blanket and handed him to me.

I looked down at my new baby boy. He burped, and then opened his tiny eyes. "Oh, my goodness, he's so gorgeous," I said. He had my face and his father's small nose. I let out a giggle. "How are you, little Joey?" I asked. I loved him from his very first burp.

On October 24, 1999, I finally settled something—there had to be a God if I could have been given a gift like this. I will always think of Joey's birth as the happiest moment of my entire life.

MY LITTLE HUGGY BEAR—that's what I called Joey most of the time. Every time I cradled my son close to my chest he just felt so warm and snuggly. So when I lifted him from the bed, I started saying, "Hello, my little huggy bear," and the nickname stuck.

Joey was the sweetest baby. Unless he was hungry or wet, he hardly ever cried. He and I shared a small bedroom on the second floor, and within just a couple of months he was sleeping through the night. I didn't have enough money for a crib, so I kept him with me in the bed, which was a twin-sized mattress stuck into a corner of the room. After carefully wrapping Joey in a blue blanket, I'd sing to him as I rocked him back and forth. One of his favorite melodies seemed to be "I Will Always Love You," the Whitney Houston hit. Whenever I sang that song, his eyes would get so big.

Joey grew fast. Because I wasn't working, I depended on Social Security checks; when I turned eighteen, they came directly to me. It wasn't enough, but at least I had a little money to buy diapers and formula. I wished I could have just breastfed Joey, but because of some medicine the doctors put me on after his birth, I couldn't.

Not long after my parents parted, Ma began seeing other men. Over time one Latino man seemed to be around our place a lot. I'll call him Carlos. He seemed like a decent enough guy—at least at first. When Joey was about six months old, Carlos moved in.

As JOEY WENT from cooing to crawling to walking, the two of us had so much fun together. He loved *101 Dalmatians*, so we'd watch that together. And he loved to sing along with me; I was always teaching him songs. He really liked "The Wheels on the Bus," so I sang that to him a lot. One evening he was playing with his toy pot and stirrer.

"What are you making, honey?" I said, smiling.

"Sketti!" he shouted, trying to say "spaghetti." Then he lifted his spoon up in the air and clapped it against his left hand. We had a joke that whenever we ate spaghetti and meatballs, he'd try to steal one of my meatballs and I'd pretend not to know where it went. He'd laugh hysterically as I looked all over for it.

Later on that night, after I bathed him, put lotion on his body, and started fastening his onesie pajamas, he jumped up and pranced around the bedroom to the beat of a song on the radio.

"Come here, huggy bear," I called out. He came back toward me so I could finish snapping on his PJs. "You're such a silly little boy!" He just grinned.

I absolutely loved sharing the holidays with Joey, especially because my family never really celebrated. During Christmas 2001 Joey was two. I took some of the money from my Social Security check and went to the local Family Dollar to buy him some presents. He kept asking for a tree. To be honest, I didn't quite have the money to purchase gifts *and* a tree, so I tried to make a little tree myself by gathering branches and leaves from the street and attaching them to a pole with super glue. It was pretty pathetic looking, but at two, Joey didn't really know the difference. "Pretty!" he said when I attached the last branch a few days before Christmas. We both just stood there and admired it.

I didn't wrap up Joey's presents until the night before Christmas. He was so excited, so I knew he'd try to sneak and open them. At midnight I began wrapping his gifts downstairs in the living room. A little after 1 A.M., I finally put the presents under the makeshift tree and cozied up next to him in bed, wondering how early he'd try to get me up.

Less than four hours later, at 5 A.M., Joey was wide awake. "Mommy, Mommy!" he said, bouncing up and down on the mattress. "Christmas!"

I turned over and buried my head underneath a pillow. "Yay, it's Christmas!" he continued shouting. "Jingle bells, jingle bells!" he sang. A couple of minutes later I dragged myself up, rubbed my eyes, and put on my glasses.

"Okay, huggy bear," I said. "Mommy is awake now." Just seeing his face so lit up was enough to get me out of bed.

We sang three verses of "O, Christmas Tree" together first—Joey just repeating the song's name over and over—and then I let him open the presents. There was paper all over that room. He screamed when he opened the first package. "Helmet!" I nodded and smiled as he put on the football helmet.

"Yes, baby," I said. "I knew you'd like that."

Then he went totally nuts when he opened another box to find a football. "Wow!" he exclaimed, widening his eyes. "More football!"

I had set out to give Joey the best Christmas ever—and before the clock even struck 6 A.M. it seemed I had pulled that off. "Thank you, Mommy!" Joey shouted as he threw his arms around my neck.

"I love you," I said, cupping his chin in my hand. "I want you to always know that." He was in total bliss, and so was I—at least until January rolled around and I realized how little money I had left after the holidays.

# 7

## Losing Joey

IN THE SPRING of 2002 I began searching for a job—*any* job. I looked every day. I was tired of being broke, and I was done with depending on my SSI check.

"Ma, will you watch Joey for me?" I'd ask so I could go pick up some applications. Sometimes she'd agree to. When she did, I went to every fast food restaurant in the city, applying for jobs. But when you're four foot two and can't even reach the cash register or the coffee machine, nobody wants to hire you. I was willing to take any kind of position, even one that paid me under the table—I knew my options were limited because I hadn't finished high school. I scoured the streets of Cleveland for weeks, but by the beginning of summer I still hadn't caught a break.

One afternoon in early June, after I'd been out looking again, I dragged myself in the front door. I'd come up empty-handed, so I decided to walk home early, around 4 P.M. When I went into one of the bedrooms on the second floor, I saw my mother's boyfriend, Carlos. He was so drunk that he was slurring his words. My mother, who I'd thought was watching Joey, was nowhere in sight.

"Come over here!" Carlos said. He lunged at me.

"Mommy, Mommy!" Joey screamed. He was so panicked that he began peeing on himself. Carlos saw this and grabbed Joey by the right leg. In one quick motion he fractured Joey's knee.

The details of what happened next are too painful to describe, so I'll just explain it briefly. After I got Joey to the hospital, I wanted to tell them the truth about how he was injured, but I was terrified that he'd be taken away from me if they thought he wasn't safe at home. So I said that he had fallen in the park. Not long after I checked him into the hospital a couple of case workers from social services huddled together in the hallway. I could hear them whispering.

"Can we talk to you, Miss Knight?" the short, fat, blonde one asked. The other had dark brown hair and looked down at me over her glasses.

My breathing slowed down. "You're going to take my son away from me, aren't you?" I said.

They didn't answer right away. "We know what happened to Joey," the blonde woman finally said, looking directly into my eyes. I began to weep. The case worker then explained that Carlos had admitted what he'd done. His sister had called the hospital and told them the true story. As she spoke, my crying intensified. "Please … don't … take … my … baby!" I managed to say through my sobs. "It's not my fault!"

Not long after, I got the horrible news from the hospital staff: once my son was released from the hospital, he would be put into foster care until they could determine that his home was a safe place for him to live.

I couldn't stop weeping. "Don't take my son!" I cried, doubling over in the hallway. The nurses looked on with pity in their eyes. I stopped crying long enough to take in the only piece of good news I heard that evening: "You can stay with him one more night," a nurse told me. Then she led me to his room.

Joey was resting in one of those high beds. His little leg was wrapped in layers of white bandages. "Mommy, Mommy!" he called out when he saw me.

I went over to the edge of the bed and squeezed his hand. "I'm right here, huggy bear," I whispered.

The nurse, sensing that I was reluctant to hold him in case I might hurt him, turned to me and said, "You don't have to be afraid. It's okay if you put him in your lap. Just be careful." I nodded, and she left.

I didn't have the heart to tell Joey that this would be our final night together, but I knew I needed to tell him something.

"Mommy is not going to see you for a while, okay?" I said in his ear. I used the back of my hand to clear away a tear that snaked its way down my left cheek.

Joey gave me a worried look. Somehow I sensed that my son knew the reality, that "a while" could turn out to be forever. Later that evening I pulled Joey close to my chest as I lay next to him. I could feel his heartbeat as he slept. *Thump. Thump. Thump.* In the dark I cried as quietly as I could.

The following morning I took Joey to the hospital's playroom. We drew a couple of pictures together as I held him in my lap. After an hour I heard the staticky sounds of walkie-talkies in the hallway. The police had come.

"Ma'am," said one of the cops, "you need to say your good-byes."

How do you say good-bye to a child who has at one time lived in your body? How do you just walk out the door? How do you explain to your son that days, months, and even years may pass before he will live with his mother again? I gave Joey a gentle hug, trying to keep my tears from spilling over onto my face. As I stood up to go, Joey began pitching a fit.

"Don't leave me, Mommy!" he howled. "Don't leave me!"

"I'm just going away for a little while," I said in the most calm tone I could muster. "We'll be back together soon." I tried to settle him down by cradling him in my arms, but he kept screaming.

"Miss, we've really gotta go," the policeman said. By the way he and the other cops had been standing aside and allowing me a little extra time, I could tell they sympathized with me. I leaned over and kissed him on the forehead. The officers then escorted me from the room.

"Mommy! Mommy!" Joey cried as I followed them down the hallway. My huggy bear was pleading for me—but I couldn't even answer.

I had been abused by a family member for years. I'd lived in a garbage can under a bridge in all kinds of weather, like an animal. But nothing could have prepared me for losing my child. It was the worst thing that had ever happened to me, ever, in all my twenty-one years. I spent the night crying, aching for my son. I wondered if he was being treated well in his new home. I wondered if he was afraid, if he was calling for me, if the foster parents would be kind and understanding, or if they would be cold. It was torture not knowing where my child was sleeping or how he was being treated. Finally I crammed my fist into my mouth so I wouldn't keep everyone else awake with my sobs.

SEVERAL DAYS LATER I walked for nearly three hours to get to a court hearing. I was willing to walk any distance to see about getting Joey back. The judge yelled at me when I arrived fifteen minutes behind schedule. "It counts against you every time you're late," she barked.

I could tell there wasn't much use in explaining that I had no car. No support. No money. No job. No desire to even keep breathing if I couldn't get my son back. For the most part I felt numb, like someone had sliced me directly through the heart.

In that hearing and over the next several appointments with social service workers I learned what I would have to do to again be considered a "fit mother": I'd have to show that I could provide a safe and secure home for my son on my own. I'd also have visitation rights, for which I'd need to show up promptly. A case worker would need to be present at all these visits, which were scheduled for once every couple of weeks.

I moved out of my mother's house and into one of the bedrooms at my cousin Lisa's place. When I was small, I didn't even know Lisa; my parents never introduced us. But when I was around sixteen, she finally came over to our house one day, and I thought she was cool and very sweet. She lived on Walton Avenue in Tremont, and she was willing to let me rent one of her rooms for just $300 a month. Her place was pretty close to where my mother and Carlos lived, but as far as I was concerned, it was worlds apart. At least I was safe. I didn't really even have the money to pay Lisa for the place: I still wasn't working. But I knew I had to do whatever it took to get away from the violent surroundings that had led to me losing Joey. *I'll take the place with Lisa and worry later about how to pay for it,* I thought. So I moved in.

Lisa, who is about ten years older than me, did her best to make me feel at home. After I'd return from job searching, she'd sometimes cook me up one of those packets of ramen noodles. She knew how depressed and alone I felt, so she asked some of our other relatives who lived nearby to introduce me around the neighborhood. One of our much younger cousins, Deanna, lived within a few blocks. On an afternoon in late June of 2002, when Deanna and I were chilling out on my front stoop, she introduced me to one of her classmates.

"Michelle, this is my girl, Emily—Emily Castro," she said. Emily nodded at me in acknowledgment. Like Deanna, Emily was around fourteen. She had dark hair and a pretty smile, and over the next several weeks she came by our place a lot. She lived just a couple of blocks away with her mother, she told me. She was seven years younger than me (although most people thought I was twelve, though I was now twenty-one), but that didn't bug me at all. She was such a friendly kid. Plus, back when I was in school, I'd gotten used to being around kids who were much younger than me because I'd fallen so far behind. And especially on those afternoons when I came home feeling very discouraged about my job search, kicking it with Emily and Deanna was one way to take my mind off of everything.

A little at a time, I got to know Emily. She told me that her parents weren't together but that she still saw her father at his house on Seymour.

"That's cool," I said.

Emily then pulled her cell from her pocket and showed me a photo of him. She mentioned that he was named Ariel, and he had a job as a bus driver. In the photo Emily's father wore a smile, one I thought was similar to hers. He had thick, dark, wavy hair, a moustache, and a goatee. He did look a little disheveled in the photo—his hair kind of stuck out from his head—but I thought that was okay.

"That's great that you still get to hang out with him," I said. Emily nodded and slipped the phone back into her purse.

Another time when Emily was with me and my cousin, she called her father on her cell and put him on speaker phone. She told him she would be ready at six. The plan was for her dad to swing by her mother's and pick her up in his truck.

"Okay," her father said in a relaxed tone of voice. "I'll be there at six."

Emily never actually introduced me to "AC," as she called him, in person, yet I felt like I kind of knew him. Several times that summer I heard the two chatting on the cell. They'd goof around with each other on loudspeaker. Her dad would talk to her in this silly hillbilly voice that he knew how to put on. He seemed like a pretty nice guy.

MY FIRST VISIT with Joey was around Fourth of July weekend, 2002, about a month after he was placed with a foster care family. The social worker had arranged to meet at a park for our one-hour visit.

"Mommy, Mommy!" he called out when I walked across the field. I swept Joey into my arms and hugged him so hard, I almost squeezed out all his breath.

"Oh, baby!" I said. I knew my visit with Joey would be too short, so for every single minute of our time together, I didn't take my eyes off of him.

On the little playground Joey and I slid down together on the kiddie slide—me in the back, with him in the front. "Wheee!" I said, holding up Joey's arms as we went down. In between our laughter, we talked.

"Are you okay, huggy bear?" I asked, a lump in my throat.

"I miss you!" Joey said. A moment later I looked up to notice the social services worker observing us closely from the other side of the playground. It felt weird to have someone watching me play with my own child, but I was determined to ignore her and just focus on my son.

When the hour was up, I had to say good-bye. It took everything I had not to grab my baby up in my arms and run down the street with him. "I don't wanna go back there. I wanna go home with you," he said.

"I know, sweetie," I said, stroking his hair, "but you can't stay with me right now. We'll get back together soon."

He clung to my leg with all his might. "No! Don't go!" he cried.

I felt like I was reliving that awful time in the hospital playroom. "I'll see you again next time, baby," I comforted him.

The social worker had to pull him off my leg and drag him, kicking and screaming, back to her car. As she put him into his car seat, I heard him wailing. Feeling like my heart was breaking in two, I stayed and watched until the car had disappeared down the street.

In mid-July I had to miss a scheduled visit with Joey. That hurt me, because I knew the court system would hold it against me. It would lengthen the time it would take for me to prove that I should have Joey returned to my care. But because I couldn't always find a ride and I had no car or driver's license, I had to walk. When Joey was first placed in the foster care system, he didn't yet have a permanent family, so he was moved around from home to home. That meant a meeting spot would sometimes be hours away by foot. I did my best to get there and be on time, but on the day I had to miss, it just wasn't possible.

THE REST OF July felt like one big, long, hot blur to me—a Sunday felt no different from a Tuesday, Wednesday, or Thursday. All I thought about was when I could next see Joey and how we could eventually be reunited. I spent every waking moment trying to do anything I could to make that possible.

For starters, I needed to find a job. In the mornings around eight I strapped on my sandals and set out on foot to put in more applications; in the late afternoons I hung out on the porch with Emily and Deanna. Sometimes Lisa and I would walk down to the convenience store and buy a beer to pass between us. Back indoors, when I could get a seat directly in front of the fan, I did. To make things even worse, my glasses fell off my face and got broken one day when I was walking on the street. Because I was very nearsighted, I was having to squint as I went around town applying for jobs. Combined with the searing heat, my blurry vision made me feel disoriented. And I definitely couldn't afford to buy a new pair of glasses. I'd just have to make do.

# 8

## Vanished

AUGUST 23, 2002, at 2:30—that's the day I was scheduled for my next appointment with social services about the process of getting Joey back and preparing for the court hearing set for August 29. The case workers had sent me an address, but I had absolutely no clue how to get there. I was counting on someone in my family to take me, so I turned down the ride social services had offered to me. I was relieved I had a way to get there—until my family member called the following morning to tell me they couldn't give me a lift after all. I automatically realized two things: I would probably get lost, and because I'd be walking, I was almost certain to be late. *Oh, God.*

I found out that I didn't have a ride at 11 A.M., which at least left me with some time to pull together a plan. "I'm pretty sure that address is downtown," she had told me. I'd need to give myself no less than one and a half to two hours to walk there from my neighborhood, plus time to find the place. I showered, threw on some knee-length jean shorts, a plain white T-shirt, and my most comfortable pair of sandals. I then shoveled down a toaster pastry.

"Will you come with me?" I asked Deanna. For whatever reason, she'd stayed home from school that day and then walked over to our place.

"Sure," she said, pulling on her sneakers. I put my brown swing pack across my body and stuffed the paper with the appointment details into its front zip pocket. At noon we headed out.

Under the hot sun we walked for about an hour before we reached the downtown area, but we couldn't locate the address. We asked everyone from a barber shop owner to a guy in a deli. Everyone just shrugged and said, "I have no idea where that is."

A little after 1 P.M. I decided I'd better stop and call the social services office. I knew I needed to let someone know I might be late. I fished out the paper from my purse, squinted at a number at the bottom of it, and then slid a quarter into the pay phone. A gruff-sounding receptionist answered.

"I don't know where the place is," I told her, "and I'm walking ..."

The woman cut me off. "Then you should've taken the ride we offered you!" she said.

"But I didn't think I needed a ride. A family member was supposed to drive me there," I explained. Then before I could ask her for detailed directions—*click*. I knew that being late would be held against me. At that point, though, I really didn't know what else to try. I was already feeling dehydrated from the heat. Circles of sweat had formed on my white T-shirt beneath my armpits. I was hungry and wiped out. And I was also furious with myself that I'd probably have to miss another appointment. *I should've taken the ride offered by social services. I should've figured out where the address was the night before.*

"Let's just turn back toward home," I said to Deanna. Her face was red and dripping sweat.

"Are you sure?" she said. "Maybe we can still find it."

"Let's just start walking again and ask some more people along the way," I suggested.

That's exactly what we did, but along our route not a single person could even halfway tell us where we should go. As we were walking past a laundromat, I looked through the glass window and noticed a clock up on the wall. It read 1:18 P.M. There wasn't much time left. I decided I should try calling the office again.

"Why don't you start heading back without me," I told Deanna. "I'll look around to see if I can find another pay phone, and then I'll catch up with you."

She nodded and began to walk home. I came across another phone booth and dialed. This time when I got through to the main menu I bypassed the evil receptionist and tried to reach my case worker directly. But you needed a special PIN number to get to any particular worker's direct line, and I didn't have it with me. I pulled the sheet from my purse and held it close to my face to try to read it, but I didn't find anything that looked like a PIN. Around 1:30 I started walking in the direction of home and looked ahead to see if I could spot my cousin. I could see a girl that I thought was her in the distance, but she was too far away to hear me calling her. So I kept walking alone. *Maybe I can still find a ride*, I told myself.

Around 2:30—the time of my scheduled appointment—I had just made it back into my neighborhood. I passed the Family Dollar store that I'd shopped in a bunch of times, the same one where I'd once gotten Joey those Christmas gifts. I was dying for something to drink. Once inside I noticed that the store seemed crowded. Making my way to the soda aisle, I noticed a nice-looking woman. *Maybe she can help me,* I thought.

"Excuse me, miss," I said, pulling out my crumpled paper, "do you happen to have any idea where this address is?" I pointed to the top of the sheet. She lowered the container of deodorant she was holding and looked at me, then at the address.

"I wish I could tell you, honey," she said, "but I'm not even from this area."

"Well, that's the thing," I said. "I don't think this address *is* in this area. It could be someplace downtown."

"Sorry," she said, placing the deodorant into her basket. "I don't think I can be much help."

Feeling hopeless, I pushed the paper into my front pocket, grabbed a soda, and lined up at the register. The cashier, a stocky blonde woman, seemed a little frazzled. After I paid, I started for the door. Then I thought, *Maybe I should ask the cashier if she knows where the address is,* and I circled back to the counter. As she was ringing up another customer, I pulled out my sheet and showed it to her.

"Excuse me. Do you know where this is?" I asked.

She eyed the address for a moment. "Actually, I think you just go right up here to the corner, then swing a left, but I'm not 100 percent positive about that," she said.

Just as I was about to leave again I heard a male voice from a few feet away. "I know exactly where that is." I turned, and when he stepped closer, I recognized the man from his photo. It was Ariel Castro, Emily's father.

"Oh, hi," I said. He stepped forward to pay for his items, a couple of screwdrivers and a can of car oil. "I'm Michelle; Emily's friend," I continued. "I know your daughter."

He smiled. "Oh, yes," he said in a soft tone, the same one I'd heard him use on the phone with his daughter. "If you give me a second here, maybe I can show you how to get there." *Thank you, God!* I'd be late, but at least I could still probably make the appointment.

As the cashier finished ringing him up, I got a better look at him. He was about as scruffy as he'd seemed in the head shot; his thick, wavy hair was uncombed and fluffed out a bit over his olive skin. His hands were rusty, like he hadn't lotioned them in months, and the skin was peeling. He looked around forty years old. His pot belly spilled out over the top of his black jeans. He wore a checkered, long-sleeved flannel shirt with a couple of grease stains on it, as if he'd been working on a car. His shirtsleeves were rolled up to his elbows. *How can he walk around with flannel on in the summer?* I wondered. He looked Mexican to me, but I knew from talking to Emily that he was from Puerto Rico. He caught me staring, and when I shifted my gaze, he smiled at me again. As ratty as he was, he seemed like a decent enough guy.

He shoved his change into his back pocket and stepped toward me in his work boots. "I'm a little turned around myself today," he said, chuckling. "Do you happen to know where there's a Key Bank?"

I did. "It's over there," I said, pointing. "Just take a right."

He nodded. "But first I'll help you find your address," he said. "Want me to give you a ride?"

"Yes," I heard myself say, but then something told me that I should probably check in with my friend to let her know I'd be accepting a ride from her father. "Um, can we call Emily first and let her know?" I asked.

When he leaned in toward me, I caught a whiff of him: he smelled like transmission fluid. "Emily's in school right now. I don't want to bother her," he said. I paused. "Well, I guess you could give me a ride," I said. "Thanks."

As we walked out the front door together, he took me by the upper arm. His grip seemed a little too tight. But not even a second later he loosened it.

"Oh, I'm so sorry!" Ariel said, laughing a little. "I was holding your arm too tight, wasn't I?" I laughed nervously and nodded, then straightened the upper sleeve on my tee. "Sometimes I don't know my own strength," he said. "Forgive me."

In that moment something seemed off, but once he apologized, I excused his strong grip as an innocent mistake. Plus, I trusted him much more than I would have trusted a complete stranger. After all, he was my friend's dad, not to mention an angel who was sent to get me to my appointment. Side by side, we walked through the other cars until he spotted his orange-ish Chevy four-door in the far corner of the lot. He came around to the passenger side and helped me in.

The inside of his truck looked as grubby as he did. Big Mac wrappers were scattered all over the floor. A couple of old Chinese food containers were wedged in a corner near the carpeted footrest on my side. The knobs to open the two front windows were both missing. "Wow, you must live in this place," I said, my eyes darting about.

He laughed. "I know, it's kinda messy. I'm such a bachelor."

He slid the key into the ignition and started the car. Then suddenly, out of nowhere, he jerked the steering wheel hard and we began spinning. "Woo-hoo!" he said. Frozen, I clutched the side of the seat. "Oh, calm down," he said when he noticed the worried look on my face. "I'm just having a little fun. I like to do that with my kids sometimes."

I giggled a little. I knew from Emily that her dad was a bit silly, like when he talked to her in a hillbilly voice. I sat back in my seat and tried to relax as we pulled out of the lot.

As we rode along and chatted, I told him about Joey, about how this appointment was so important because I wanted to get him back. "I miss him so much," I said. Ariel nodded sympathetically. Right then, even though I couldn't see the streets very well without my glasses, I noticed we didn't seem to be heading back downtown, where my appointment was.

"Where are we going?" I asked.

"Oh, I just need to stop by my house for a minute and pick up some stuff," he said. "Emily should be home soon—school just got out. I can give her some money, and maybe you two can go to the mall together later on. But don't worry. First I'll take you to your appointment."

I looked over at him. "Okay," I said, "but I really can't stay that long. I'm already late. I need to get to that appointment or else I'm going to be in big trouble. Emily and I can go to the mall another day." The clock on his dashboard read 3 P.M., so I knew Emily ought to be home in a few minutes.

"It won't be too long," he said. "I promise."

We rode along for another minute while he talked about how much he loved motorcycles and how he was trying to sell one. "I might know someone who'd like to buy it from you," I said, thinking of a guy who lived in my neighborhood.

He then shifted the topic: "Hey, do you like puppies?" he asked.

"Oh, I love them!" I said. "And so does my son." Every time we used to run into a dog on the street Joey would get really excited and want to pet it.

"I've actually got some puppies at my place," Ariel said. "My dog had babies a while back. When we stop there, maybe I can give you one. Then when you get Joey back, you can give him a puppy. I bet he'd like that."

*What a nice idea—Joey would love to have a puppy*, I thought. *That would make a great coming-home present.*

On Seymour Avenue we slowed down in front of a white, two-level house that was within blocks of where I lived—I recognized the street. Surrounding the house was an eight-foot chain-link fence.

"We're here," he announced.

I looked into the front yard to see even more trash than there was in his truck—lots of newspapers and empty aluminum soda cans. The yellowing grass clearly hadn't been cut in days, maybe even decades. To get to his place we'd driven for at least seven minutes, and yet we both lived just a two-minute drive away from Family Dollar. *Did we just go around in circles or something?* I thought.

He got out of the car and opened a gate that led to a driveway along the house. He then hopped back in and shifted the vehicle into reverse, looked back over his shoulder, and slowly backed into the driveway. A van was parked further back in the yard. Afterward he locked the gate with a big padlock—and that made me nervous.

"Why are you parking and locking the gate?" I asked. "I thought we were just stopping for a minute."

"Because this is a terrible neighborhood," he shot back. "I don't want my truck to get stolen."

*Why would anyone want this piece of crap?* I thought to myself.

From the window of the truck, in the trash-littered backyard, I could see a reddish-brown furry Chow Chow on a chain. "Aw, she's cute!" I said.

"Her name is Maxine," he said.

"Why isn't she in the house with her puppies?"

"I have to take her outside because sometimes she pees in the house," he explained. That didn't quite make sense to me—hadn't he housetrained the dog when she was just a puppy?—but whatever. I didn't make much of it. "I'll be right back," he said. He got out of the car but left the motor running.

Less than a minute later Ariel returned and opened my side of the door. "Why don't you come in for a sec," he said.

I wrinkled my nose. "Why?"

"Because then you can pick out your own puppy," he said. Noting my hesitation, he pressed on. "You don't have to be nervous," he said. "Emily's here. Just come in for a sec and see the puppies."

I drew a breath, and in a moment I'll regret for the rest of my life, I finally said, "Okay—just for a minute."

He helped me down from the truck and we walked toward his wooden back door. Just before I stepped inside I saw an old white man in the neighboring yard. I recognized him from the area; his kids were brats. I waved and yelled out "Hello!" He gave me a hard stare and then waved back. The exchange immediately put me at ease. *He has neighbors that know him,* I thought. *And Emily is here. I'm being ridiculous.*

If Ariel's truck and yard were a hot mess, they were nothing compared to his house. Sheets of newspaper were all over the kitchen and in the living room that was just beyond it. Crusted-over dirty dishes were stacked in the sink. Beer bottles were everywhere. It smelled like a mix of piss, beer, and rotten black beans. A lot of the windows were boarded up from the inside. *How could his daughter stand to visit here?* I thought. I wondered if Emily felt as grossed out as I did.

"Welcome," Ariel said, motioning me to step farther into the kitchen. "Come on in. Like I said, I'm a bachelor. I don't get a chance to clean up much."

I didn't speak—I just gawked. I followed him into the living room, wondering how I could hurry up and get out of this smelly pit without seeming rude. I saw a photo resting on top of a large TV, which was right next to a fireplace mantel. "Aw, I love that picture of Emily—she looks so cute," I said. "You said she's here?"

He nodded. "She's right downstairs, putting some laundry in the machine," he assured me. "She'll be up in a minute. Why don't you come with me upstairs so you can go ahead and pick out a puppy?" He pointed to a staircase off the living room.

"Uh-uh—I'm not going up there," I said, backing up a step.

"C'mon," he said, "you really don't have to be afraid. It's me, AC—Emily's dad."

*That's true,* I thought. *I'm probably just being silly.* I didn't want Ariel to tell Emily I'd acted like I was afraid of him. Besides that, I could already just see Joey's face if he came

76

home to the surprise of having his own puppy. "I could try to bring the puppies downstairs," he said, "but I don't want them running around loose down here."

I studied his face. He seemed so sincere. So, a beat later, I caved. I overrode my reluctance, put my right foot on the bottom stair, and began walking up. He followed from behind, his heavy stomps sounding like an elephant.

About halfway up to the top of the staircase, I still didn't hear any barking. "How come I don't hear the puppies?" I said.

"They're probably asleep," he said. "They're so little, they spend half the day snoozing. Wait 'til you see them—they're so cute when they're all snuggled up together."

They sounded adorable; I couldn't wait to hold one. At the top of the stairs there was a room. "They're right through there, in a box," he said. We stepped through the bedroom with white walls, and continued into a connected room that was pink.

"The puppies are underneath the dresser," he said. I looked down to where he was pointing and then, suddenly—*Slam!*—he closed the door.

"Let me out of here!" I screamed. "Oh, please—let me out! I've gotta get to my appointment!"

He slapped his big hand over my mouth and nose and pressed his other hand against the back of my skull. "I'll kill you if you scream again!" he yelled.

The man I'd first met at Family Dollar—that gentle guy who'd talked on the phone with Emily and who'd seemed so nice to me—had suddenly turned into a madman. He yanked my hands behind me and pushed me to the ground.

In that moment a whole string of memories from the last two decades filled my head. The back of our ugly brown station wagon. My family's canary-yellow house. My blue trash can under the bridge. Arsenio's warm smile. Sniper and Roderick playing pool with me in the basement. Joey's giggling and my fake tree during our final Christmas together. I closed my eyes and tried to prepare myself for what might happen next. To this day I still cannot believe what did.

# 9

# Trapped

"DON'T MOVE!" THE dude shouted in my face as I lay on the
floor. His spit flew into my eyes and his breath stank like
beer. He grabbed my purse and threw it into a corner of the
pink room. "I'm coming right back!" He ran into the next
room, and I could hear him looking for something in the
closet. I tried to scream, but when I opened my mouth, no
sound came out. And I mean *none*. My hands shook like I was
caught in an earthquake.

I was in a full-blown panic. My body was paralyzed, but my
mind was going crazy. *Come on, girl, you've gotta do something!* I
thought. My eyes fell upon two metal poles, one on each side
of the room. A wire was strung between them, like a clothes-
line. Not even a second later the dude was back, lifting a
heavy stool through the door. He set it down next to me. In
his hand he had two orange extension cords. My heart was
beating so hard, it felt like it was about to fall out of my chest.
I started to struggle up to my feet.

"Lay still!" he yelled.

I gagged and almost threw up. He sat on the stool and grabbed both of my legs. I went wild, thrashing around and trying to fight him off, but he was too strong for me. He wrapped one cord so tightly around my ankles that it cut into my skin. He didn't say a single word while he was tying me up, but he was breathing hard. My brain was going nuts: *How could this be happening to me? How do I get out of here?* As he went around and around my ankles with that cord, sweat dripped down his chin and onto my shirt. It smelled like a nasty mix of pee and car oil.

After he tied up my feet, I couldn't feel them anymore. He yanked my arms behind me as I screamed and tried to punch him in the face.

"Please, just let me go!" I begged him, tears running down my face.

"Shut up or I'll really kill you!" he shouted.

He wrapped my wrists together and pulled my hands and feet together in back with the cord. Then he looped the cord around my neck.

"Stop it!" I tried to yell. But the cord was cutting off my air. As I lay there tied up on the floor, I figured he was about to hook me to one of those poles. But he suddenly unzipped his jeans, pulled down his pants, and whipped out his penis. His gut hung down below his flannel shirt, and he wasn't wearing any underwear.

"You're only going to be here with me for a little while," he said as he started jerking off. Every time he moved, his jeans fell down a little more. The harder he pumped, the more he ran his mouth. "I really just want us to be friends," he said. "My wife and kids left, and all I want is for someone to be here for me. I need you."

80

My pulse was going out of control. My hands and feet were numb, and my face was wet from all the tears. Snot was running down my nose. I had been scared crapless many times before, but nothing came close to the terror I felt as I lay on that floor. I was sure I was about to die. *Oh God, why is this happening to me?*

Desperate, I opened my eyes and looked up at the window. Right then the dude pointed himself right at me. "*Yeees!*" he screamed out. A big glob of semen sprayed all over my shorts.

He sat down on the stool, and for the longest time he just rested. His jeans had slid all the way down to his ankles. He leaned his head against the pink wall and took a bunch of deep breaths.

"Now I need you to be still so I can put you up on these poles," he finally said. He got up and pulled up his pants. Then he started taking off my sandals. I began praying the only prayer I knew. "Now ... I lay me ... down to sleep," I said. "I pray ... the Lord ... my soul to keep ..."

"Stop making noise!" he shouted. "No one can hear you!" But I kept on praying. "If I should die ... before I wake ..." He smacked me hard on the side of the head, and I got real quiet.

He threw my sandals into the corner with my purse. Then he rolled me over onto my stomach as I tried to squirm out of his reach. He tied the second orange cord to the one around my hands, feet, and neck. Then he hoisted my body up to the long wires between the two poles and tied the cord behind my back to the wires. When he was done, I was raised up off the floor by about twelve inches, facing the window. It felt like he was hanging me up for show—like a trophy on a wall. A minute later he stuffed a stinky gray sock in my mouth and put duct tape all the way around my head to keep it in place. Through the sock, all I could do was moan—and hope that someone would hear me.

"I'm gonna get us some food," he said in a very calm voice. Mr. Hyde had suddenly gone away, and Dr. Jekyll was there to take his place. "You stay right where you are," he said. "Don't leave. And don't make a sound."

*How am I going to make a sound when you have my mouth taped shut?* I thought frantically. He turned on the radio that was sitting on the dresser and cranked up the volume so loud that it hurt my eardrums. Then he slammed the door and stomped down the stairs.

Over the noise of the radio I heard his truck's engine rev up. I thought maybe I could undo the cords, so I started swinging myself back and forth. But all I did was make myself very dizzy. From where I was hanging, I could see other people's windows across the street. *Can anyone see me?* I thought. Since I didn't have my glasses, I couldn't see very well. I tried to scream again, but I was pretty sure no one could hear me over the thumping noise of rapping from the radio.

I looked around the room to see if I could reach something that could help me escape, but that was impossible because of the way he had tied me up. I could see a few girls' clothes through the open closet door. I remembered that Emily had told me about her little sister, Rosie, so this must have been her room before their mother moved them out. There was a picture of a mermaid lying on the floor. It looked like it was painted by a kid. Under the mermaid it said "Ariel." Maybe his daughter made that for him. How could a man with two daughters, and one that I was friends with, do this to me? Emily seemed to think her father was okay—did she have no idea he was a pervert? I knew now that he'd lied about her being in the house, but maybe she'd come over later. Had Deanna gone back home and told everyone I had vanished? My mind raced as I hoped to God that somebody was already out looking for me.

As TIME WENT BY I went from feeling numb to feeling like someone was sticking a thousand pins and needles all over my body. My head started throbbing from the loudness of the radio. By the time the sun went down the psycho hadn't returned. I had started to feel pretty sure that when he did come back, he was going to kill me. All I could think about was my sweet Joey—and if I would ever see him again.

Morning came, then afternoon, then another night passed. He left me hanging there for *what seemed like more than a day*. My belly ached from hunger. I was thirstier than I'd ever been in my whole life, and my mouth was unbelievably dry with the sock crammed into it. I smelled bad because I had peed on myself. Twice. And I had passed out a few times with that cord choking me. If he was ever back in the house during that time, I never heard it. I was probably out cold, or maybe I couldn't hear it because the radio was so loud. When he finally barged in the door, he was holding some kind of sandwich in a yellow McDonald's wrapper.

"You've gotta eat something," he said. He turned down the radio. Then he suddenly ripped the duct tape from my head and removed the sock. Some of my hair came off with the tape and I screamed, it hurt me so bad. He took the wrapping off the sausage sandwich and tried to shove it into my face, but I pressed my lips together and shook my head from side to side. Then he grabbed me by the jaw and tried to force it in.

"You need to eat!" he shouted.

*What if he's put drugs in the food? What if he's going to poison me?* I kept my lips closed as tightly as I could until he finally threw the sandwich down.

He undid the cord that was attached to the wire, and I crashed painfully onto the floor. I started crying again and tried to sit up. My limbs were so numb, I couldn't feel them.

"Lay still, you little slut," he said. With one hand he unwound the cord around my neck, and with the other he held me down. When he unwrapped the cord from my ankle, a stream of blood ran down my foot.

"I need you to get up," he said.

"Are you serious? I can't even stand up!" I shouted.

Before I could say another word, he picked me up and slung me over his shoulder. Grunting, he carried me into the small white room next door. Over in the corner there was a stained queen-size mattress with no sheets. He slammed me down on the mattress and stripped off all my clothes. For the next hour straight, as I screamed nonstop, he raped me. And then again. And again. And again. He hurt me so bad that the mattress was soaked with my blood. At first I tried to kick him off and scratch his face with my fingernails, but there was no way my small body could fend off such a big man.

"Please don't hurt me anymore," I said, sobbing, when it looked like maybe he was slowing down. I thought that if I tried to sound sweet, he might let me go. "I just want to get back home," I told him. "I don't think you're a bad person—

you just made this one mistake. If you let me go now, we can forget about this."

But at that point he laid his sweaty naked body down next to me and started talking, almost like he thought I was his girlfriend.

"I really wish I didn't have to do this to you," he said quietly. He sighed and even started to cry a little. Dr. Jekyll was back.

"My wife left me. I didn't mean to beat her, but it's like I ain't got the power to stop myself." I stared at him. "I got molested when I was a little kid. And nobody did nothin' about it. That's why I started jerking off. That's why I started watching porn. I just want one person to stay here with me."

While he went on and on with this nonsense, I kept my eye on the door. I was hoping I could somehow make a fast break down the stairs. But because of the way he had me trapped in the corner of the mattress, I couldn't get around him. I didn't say a word at first. But then I said, "Why don't you get a girlfriend? Just because you had a bad life doesn't mean you have to do this kind of stuff. Lots of people have had tough childhoods."

He didn't look at me. Suddenly he jumped off the bed, picked up his jeans, and pulled some cash out of one of the pockets. "There's your payment for your services," he said, throwing down a few dollar bills. After that he left the room.

My *payment?* I had no idea what he was talking about. He went across the hall. I stumbled to my aching feet, but before I could reach the door he was back. "Where do you think you're going?" he said. I backed up onto the mattress.

He was holding my purse. He turned it upside down and emptied everything onto the floor. "How old are you?" he asked. I didn't answer. "What's your birth date?" I still didn't say a word. So he got down and searched through all of my stuff until he found my wallet. He pulled out my ID and stared at it for a long time. "You're twenty-one?" he said.

I shook my head yes.

He stared at me. "I thought you was much younger!" he shouted. "I thought you was a prostitute!" *I guess he thought I was a hooker. Maybe that's why he was throwing money at me. Maybe he'll let me get out of here now.* He was so pissed off that he threw the ID across the room. After a minute he came over and sat on the edge of the mattress. "Look, you and I are just gonna be friends, okay?" he said. My hands started to shake. "You're not gonna be here with me no real long time. Just maybe till Christmas."

I could feel myself getting dizzy. *Christmas? There's no way in the world I can be here till Christmas!* I started to cry, and the truth of what was happening hit me like a thousand knives in my gut. *Oh my God. I am trapped here in this psychopath's house.*

"First I gotta see if I can trust you." He gave me my shirt and underwear but not my shorts. He stared at me as I put them on. My tan underwear, the pair I loved because they had butterflies on them, were wet with pee and stained with blood. My shirt still smelled like his vile sweat.

After I was dressed, he put his hand on my arm. I pushed him away, but he yanked me by the hair and pulled me up from the bed.

"No!" I screamed. "Let me go!"

He just ignored me and dragged me over to the top of the staircase. I didn't know where he was taking me, but I couldn't imagine that it could be much worse than what he'd just put me through. I was wrong.

# 10

# The Dungeon

CREAK. CREAK. CREAK. He dragged me down the old wooden stairs to the first floor and stopped for a minute. Then he pulled me over to another door and undid a padlock. It led to a staircase, one that was going down. *The basement—that's where he's taking me!* My whole body started to shake. Just thinking about going to the basement scared the shit out of me. In all the horror books I'd ever read, nothing good ever happened in the basement. *This might be my last stop.* I held my breath, closed my eyes real tight for a second, and tried to imagine I was with my huggy bear.

Once we got down there, it was pretty dark. He shoved me down the last steps and threw me on the floor. There was just barely enough light for me to see that I was on top of a big pile of dirty men's clothes. The pile was right next to a fat pole that went all the way from the floor to the ceiling. After he turned on a ceiling lightbulb, I could see better. "Stay right there," he told me. He went to another part of the room. That gave me a minute to look around at the place where I might wind up being murdered.

The whole room was covered with junk. A bunch of rusted chains were strewed everywhere. Piles of dirty clothes were all over the place. There was a big sink with a puddle of water on the floor underneath it and an old washing machine right next to it. I saw a couple of cabinets, one blue, one white. Tools and pipes were scattered all around. Boxes were stacked up almost to the ceiling. And whole lot of videos. *That must be his porn stuff,* I thought. The place smelled like rot and mildew. There was a very small window on the same side of the house as his driveway. You couldn't see out of it because it was covered with black dirt; no light came through. On the basement door were a bunch of alarms. There were so many wires sticking out from the alarms that I figured he had rigged them up himself.

At that moment the dude leaned down and picked up two rusty chains. They were the longest ones I'd ever seen, at least eight feet. Even though he was holding up a big section of them, a lot of the links were still piled up by his feet.

I was crying uncontrollably, like a baby. My eyes were almost swollen shut. "Please, please—just let me go!" I screamed. But he didn't bat an eyelash, and I was too far under the ground for anyone to hear me.

"How do you think I'm supposed to trust you if you keep making that kind of noise?" he said. I kept right on sobbing. "Sit over there by the pole!" he shouted. I scooted over to it. He pulled my arms behind me and put some kind of twisty bands on my wrists. After stuffing another sock into my mouth, he pushed me against the pole and started wrapping the huge chains all the way around my stomach, my neck, and the pole. *One circle. Two circles. Three circles. Four.* On the fifth time around the chain went right into my mouth.

It tasted like an old penny. *Click. Click.* He locked the two chains together behind me. *This is the end,* I thought.

"Now we have to make sure nobody can hear you," he said. He walked over and picked up something from a table. It was a motorcycle helmet. He raised it up and rammed it down over my head. I could barely breathe—and that's when everything went black.

I HAD NO CLUE what day it was when I woke up. It was totally dark. All I knew was that the dude was nowhere in sight—and the house was real, real quiet. *Is it day? Is it night?* Honestly, I couldn't tell you. But somehow I was still alive—or at least halfway alive. My brain was pretty groggy because it was very hard to get much oxygen under that heavy helmet. But I wasn't too out of it to look for a way to escape. I started moving my hands. *Maybe I can get these ties off.* They wouldn't budge. But with every bit of strength I could find, I kept trying. And trying.

Those bands were cutting into my wrists, and after working for about two hours, I was ready to give up. That's when a miracle happened: suddenly one of the twists felt a little looser. I couldn't believe it. *Maybe I can get loose!* I worked my hands like crazy, and the twisty band came all the way off. Quickly I used my free hand to undo the other twist.

Even though my body was still chained, now I could take off that nasty helmet. It was amazing to be able to breathe freely, even if it was the stale air of the filthy basement. I rubbed my arms to get some feeling back into them. I looked around, but there was nothing nearby that I could use to try to cut through the chain. I reached behind the pole and felt for one of the padlocks. *If I can just work it free …* I tried to jiggle the top part up and down. It seemed to give a tiny bit. *Oh my God—I might actually break out of here*, I thought.

Frantically I wiggled the lock. The only trouble was that even if I got this chain off, the other one was still around my stomach, and if I got that off, I would still have to get past the door alarm. I pushed my back against the pole as hard as it would go, and the chains loosened a little. I yanked and yanked on the lock. Then I heard the sound of a truck pulling into the driveway. *He's back!* Quickly I put the helmet on my head and tried to wrap the twisty bands around my hands again, the way they were before he left.

Not even two minutes later the dude's footsteps pounded down the stairs. He flipped on the light. "Why did you take off those bands?" he shouted. "I thought I could trust you, but now you're gonna have to be punished." He picked up a pipe and waved it in my face. "If you scream," he told me, "I'm gonna shove this right down your throat." I didn't make a sound. He unlocked the chains, took off the helmet, and ripped off my shirt and underwear.

What happened over the next three hours is still hard for me to think about. He didn't just rape me the way he had upstairs. He murdered my heart—or at least the small part that was still left after what I went through when I was a girl. He forced me to do things that are too painful for me to describe, things that I had never done and would never do again. I couldn't scream. I couldn't pray. I couldn't even ask God to help me get back to Joey. I was in so much shock and fear that all I could do was lie there like I was dead. In a way, I think a part of you has to die in order to get through a thing like that. It's the only way a person can survive it.

When he was finished, he kicked me over onto my back. He threw some more dollar bills at me. "I'll be paying you for your time here," he said. "I'll keep it for you in there." He pointed toward the washing machine. Then he stood and looked down at me for a long time. My lips were trembling. My eyes were puffy. Sweat and blood were pouring from me. I turned my head to the wall so I didn't have to look that monster right in the face. After a few minutes he finally spoke.

"This is where you're going to stay until you show me I can trust you," he told me. "Then maybe you can move upstairs." He chained me to the pole again and pushed the helmet over my head. On the way out, he turned off the light. In the pitch black I just sat there. Broken. Alone. *I'm going to die down here. I'll never hold my Joey again.*

I was so beaten up and exhausted that I was fading again. I leaned against the pole and tried to breathe a little better in the heavy helmet. I prayed this was all a horrible nightmare that I would soon wake up from.

I OPENED MY EYES to the sound of footsteps. *Pound. Pound. Pound.* Through the thickness of the helmet I could hear the dude come into the basement. After those first hours, I never used his real name again. I didn't think a monster deserved to have a real name, so I only called him "dude."

Roughly he yanked off the helmet. He was wearing a blue T-shirt and some raggedy sweatpants. I figured it might be morning because he didn't have on those same filthy jeans he did before. He was carrying a plate of food and a glass. He put them down on a table and came closer to me. He smelled like rotting fish.

"You've gotta eat something or you're gonna die," he said.

*So* now *you're worried about me dying?* I thought. *What a moron!*

"I know you don't want to eat the food I'm bringing you, but I'll prove it's okay," he continued. He stuck the plate of food under my nose. It was spaghetti with red sauce on top of it. "My mother made it," he said. "See, look—I'll eat some first." He used his fork to pick up some pasta and stuffed it in his mouth. "See," he said, chewing with his mouth wide open. "It's okay." Some of the sauce spilled out of the corner of his mouth. I thought he was trying to play a trick on me. But I was starving. How many days had it been since I'd eaten that toaster pastry the morning I'd left for my appointment?

When he put the fork up to my mouth, I took a little baby bite. It actually tasted decent. When he saw I was eating it, he put a lot more noodles on the fork and shoved them into my mouth. I chewed it up slowly at first, but then faster. He gave me more and more until I cleaned the whole plate. *Maybe I'm going to die,* I thought, *but at least I'm not going down on an empty stomach.* After the food was gone, he got the glass off the table. "Here's some water," he said, holding it up to my lips. I drank it so fast that I almost choked.

This time before he left, he undid my chains and made them a little looser so I could reach the toilet. By "toilet," I really mean a green bucket. He put that bucket down close to the pole. "Use this when you have to go," he said. He walked around the basement for a minute and came back with a piece of cardboard. He threw it down on top. Maybe he thought that was supposed to keep the smell inside. But I was still glad to have some way to go to the bathroom. After your life is stolen from you, even the most basic stuff makes you grateful.

WHEN YOU'RE LIVING in the dark, you lose track of time. *Is it Monday? Friday? Tuesday? Sunday? How many days have I been here?* Because you can barely see a thing, everything you hear and smell becomes a clue. When I heard the dude's phone alarm go off upstairs, I figured out that it must be morning, because right after that I could smell coffee. When I first got into the house, I wasn't sure where he slept, but I could hear his alarm, so I knew it must be on the main floor. On my way in on the first day I thought I'd seen a little room just off the kitchen. That could have been his room. Every now and then I could hear the water come on in the pipes, like he was taking a shower or washing up. I don't think he did that very often; maybe about once a week. He always stank.

The next sound I heard was the back door closing and his truck backing out of the driveway. About twenty minutes after that, the truck returned, the basement door swung open, and he came pounding down the stairs. He didn't say too much to me—he just fed me an Egg McMuffin and made me drink some OJ. On some days that was my only meal. *So when he leaves out of the driveway*, I thought, *he must be going to McDonald's.* He went there on most mornings. That's how the basement floor got covered with yellow wrappers.

Most of the time when he came downstairs in the mornings, he was dressed in a uniform: a burgundy shirt, black pants, and black combat boots. I remembered that Emily had told me her dad was a school bus driver, so whenever he had on that uniform, I knew he must be on his way to work. Soon after, I could hear him start the engine of the van. From that tiny window in the basement I could always hear what was happening in the driveway. Several hours after that I heard the van pull back in and the house door open, so he was home from work. Not long afterward I heard the sounds of people having sex, and I figured out that he was watching porn. Other times he blasted Spanish music. In both cases, he put the volume up really loud.

A couple of hours after that he usually came down to the basement wearing a flannel shirt and jeans. He often smelled like rum or beer or weed. He smoked a lot of marijuana: I could smell it all over the house. When he got to the bottom of the stairs, he sometimes had his jeans unzipped and his junk out. He was usually hard, like he had already been playing with himself. If all of these things happened one right after the other, I knew it had to be after work.

Nighttime—that's when he always did the worst stuff to me. At the end of the day, whenever I heard his boots coming down the stairs, I tried to prepare myself for the next three or four hours of torture, but there's really no way to prepare for hell. The only way I could get through it was to pretend it wasn't happening.

At night or on the weekends sometimes he showed up with a little more food. It could be anything, but it was usually something that had sat around, like dried-up pizza, spoiled beans with hard white rice, warm runny yogurt, or a stale taco. It was all total crap.

"If you wanna eat again today," he'd say, "then you'd better do what I tell you." Before I could even take a bite, he would unlock the chains, jerk me over to the pile of dirty clothes, and do the most disgusting things to me. As he did, I tried to switch my mind over to something that made me happy. *Anything.* Sometimes I thought about the Christmas when I got Joey the football. Or the day when Roderick gave me that pretty scarf. Or that time when my cousin, April, and I had so much fun roller-skating. Or how much I missed the taste of french fries from Arby's. I also thought of music I liked. "The wheels on the bus go round and round … round and round … round and round," I sang softly. Singing it made me remember Joey's sweet smile and his cute button nose. Other times I hummed "Lift Every Voice and Sing" or "Angel of Mine," that beautiful song from the gospel choir at the Baptist church I went to when I lived under the bridge. The dude was so busy torturing me that he didn't even notice the noise I was making.

On a lot of nights I ran out of good stuff to sing or think about before the pounding stopped. After he zipped up his pants, he usually sat down and started talking trash. "Nobody is even looking for you," he told me with a cruel smirk. "There ain't been any fliers put around the neighborhood, and nothin's been on the news. I can do whatever I want to you. No one gives a crap."

I tried to act like I wasn't listening, but his words shattered me into a million pieces. I hated him for saying what he said. I hated it even more that I had a feeling he might be right. *Was* anyone looking for me? Lots of people in Family Dollar would have seen me leaving with him; if my family put fliers around the neighborhood, why didn't anyone recognize my picture and tell the cops I'd gone with him in his truck? It made me feel even worse, if that was possible, that maybe no one *was* looking for me.

Every week I had one more clue about which day it could be. One time, while he was drunk and talking too much, he told me that he was in some kind of Spanish band with some other dudes.

"I play the guitar. The band is really good." He smiled like he'd won a Grammy or something.

I wanted to scream, "Do I look like I give a damn about your stupid band?" There I was, chained to a pole in a nasty basement in dirty, bloody clothes, red marks all over my body from the chains, my arms and legs tattooed with bruises from his beatings—how could the bastard think I gave a shit about his freaking band? But I just shrugged my shoulders.

Then one evening a couple of weeks later, he said, "The guys in the band are coming over tonight. You'd better not make a sound." I'm pretty sure that was a Saturday because, after five days in a row of wearing his bus driver uniform, it was the first day he didn't have it on.

Later that night I heard Maxine barking in the yard. She always went crazy whenever someone came near the house. Then I heard voices—probably around five or six, but I couldn't be sure. It sounded like the men were saying stuff in fast Spanish. Then, after a few minutes, I started hearing music. It sounded like they were playing the drums, a tambourine, and a guitar. They all started singing real loud together, also in Spanish. Even if I could have let out a scream from under that helmet, there was no way any of those guys could hear me. The music was way too loud, and I was too far away from them. As best as I could tell, those guys came over just about every Saturday. That's another way I could tell it was the first day of the weekend. But to be honest, it didn't really matter that much which day it was. All my days ended in the exact same painful way.

WHAT DO YOU DO after you spend so many hours alone in the dark? You start to go a little crazy, that's what you do. Sometimes I would talk to Joey like he was right there in the basement with me. "How are you doing, my little huggy bear?" I said. "Come give Mommy a kiss." A lot of the time I wracked my brain for ways I could get out of the chains, but after the first day, when I got the twisty bands off, the dude made sure I couldn't get them off again. So there was nothing I could do but sit there in the dark and try to keep myself from going crazy. I slept for many hours. If I thought he had gone to work, I pounded the back of my helmet against the pole and rattled the chains, hoping a neighbor would hear the noise and call 911. In between, I prayed a lot—like, for hours on end. I remembered the Bible verse the minister in the Baptist church often read:

*Although I walk through the valley of the shadow of death,*
*I will fear no evil: for thou art with me ...*

*If the neighbors can't hear me screaming, maybe God can,* I thought. But as the days turned into weeks and the weeks into months, I began to wonder if God had forgotten me too.

He kept me down in that basement for what seemed like months. I tried to keep a count of the days in my head. *One day. Seven days. Thirteen. Thirty-three. Sixty-one. Ninety.* It went from wicked hot days to much colder days. And because I was only eating once or twice a day, I lost a lot of weight. Every week he had to tighten the chains.

The entire time I was in the basement I never got to wash up or take a shower. When my period came, he'd throw a few paper napkins on the floor in front of me. "Use these," he said. I tried to roll them up and turn them into something like a tampon, but he never gave me enough, so I had brown blotches of dried blood all over my body. I also had so much of his dried semen in my hair that when I touched it, it was hard as a rock.

The whole basement smelled like a toilet because the dude hardly ever emptied that green bucket. I still had on the same T-shirt and underwear that I was wearing on the day he kidnapped me. My panties were so filthy that when he did turn on the light, I couldn't see the beautiful butterfly print anymore. I was just barely alive on the outside, and on the inside I was cracking apart.

Off and on, I was so exhausted that I'd fall asleep. Sometimes I'd dream about Joey, and it was always the same dream. He'd be taking bouncy little steps toward me, but suddenly someone would grab his arm and start pulling him away. I'd try to reach out for him, but I was paralyzed, unable to move. As he was pulled from me, he began fading away, like he was going to disappear. I'd start to scream his name—and then I'd wake up.

And every single time I woke up reality smacked me in the head all over again. I'd open my eyes and remember that I was in the dude's basement. I'd feel the chains biting into my flesh. I sank into despair when I tried yet again to work my hands out of the bindings and realized that I couldn't get free.

My stomach growling; I'd have fantasies of eating my favorite foods. I'd picture a large order of Arby's fries with hot sauce, sizzling hot and smelling like heaven. In my mind I'd take my time, nibbling little bites of each long, delicious fry until the whole container was gone. Or I'd go back to some of those meals at the church—the creamy mac and cheese melting on my tongue, the crunch of the crispy chicken skin between my teeth. Or those buttermilk biscuits, soft as a pillow, with a golden yellow pat of butter dissolving in the middle.

In my imagination I'd get so into the food that when I opened my eyes, it took me a minute to realize I wasn't in the basement at the Baptist church, surrounded by all those nice ladies offering me a second helping. Instead, I was in the filthy basement of a sicko who was worse than any of the villains I'd read about in those horror stories.

*In fact,* I realized, *I'm* living *in a horror story.*

# 11

## Lobo

"I'M TAKING YOU upstairs today." The crazy dude stood over me in the dim light of the basement. He wasn't wearing his uniform, so I figured it must be the weekend. I had heard him coming down the stairs as usual that morning, and I thought he was there for the routine—giving me some food. I was still half-asleep inside my helmet, so when I heard him speak, it caught me by surprise. He unlocked my chains and ordered me to stand up. Pins and needles prickled my legs as the blood rushed to my feet; I felt queasy and grabbed onto the pole for balance.

"Follow me," he said.

I started to get excited. *Is he going to let me go, after all?* He'd mentioned letting me go at Christmas; had I been there longer than I thought? *Maybe he finally trusts me,* I thought. *Maybe I can make it out of here after all!*

"Get moving," he said, grabbing my arm and jerking me away from the pole.

I could hardly budge after being chained up for so long, but I managed to take one step forward. He didn't say a word about why he was suddenly moving me, and I knew it would be foolish to ask. His hand gripping my arm, I followed him to the stairs, wading through the balled-up fast food wrappers and greasy tools. Then I followed him up the steps, holding onto the wall for balance.

When we got to the top of the stairs, he opened the door. *Sunlight!* I put both of my hands in front of my face. When you see daylight for the first time after a long time in the dark, it really burns your eyes! I stopped walking for a minute once I stepped into the kitchen, and for some reason he let me stop. Everything was pretty blurry, and I felt dizzy at first, until my eyes got used to all that light. It was warmer in the kitchen too, after the cold of the basement. I rubbed my arms in my thin T-shirt.

"We're going up to the bedroom," he said. He pointed toward the staircase, and I got scared, thinking about what could be waiting for me up there this time. I figured if he was going to kill me, he'd probably do it in the basement, but the dude was such a whackjob that nothing he did made sense. My teeth started to chatter as he pushed me up the stairs ahead of him.

We went back to the pink room, where he'd strung me up on the first day. The poles were gone, and an old mattress was in the corner. On the side of it was a bucket with a piece of cardboard on top; I knew what that was for. A very long chain with a padlock was on the bed. It looked like he had drilled some holes into the wall near the top of the bed and put that huge chain through it.

"Get over there," he said, pushing me down onto the mattress. He wrapped the chain around my body several times and then attached it to the radiator near the bed. The chain was so tight around me that all I could do was sit up or lie down—but not stand.

"This is where you're gonna be for a while," he told me. I wanted to spit in his face, but I knew that that would get me sent right back to the basement. At least upstairs I had light.

After checking the chain, he yanked down his jeans and raped me again.

"Why are you doing this to me?" I asked, sobbing and trying to push him away. "Please stop! You don't have to do this! Please let me go!"

"Shut up!" he yelled.

"Just let me go! Let me see my son!" I cried.

"Why should I do anything for your kid?" he said, holding me down.

"Because I'm your daughter's friend!" I said, trying to get him to listen to me.

"She'll hate me if she finds out what I've done," he said. Then he put his big hand over my mouth and kept abusing me. He was so heavy and I was so small; I didn't stand a chance of pushing him off of me.

When it was over, he started talking—a whole lot more than he ever talked down in the basement. He laid his heavy body across the mattress and got so close to me, I could feel his bad breath on my face. I was thinking, *Dude—I'm not your woman!* That was the craziest thing about the idiot: one minute he was smacking me in the head or forcing me to do horrible things; the next minute he was acting like we were great friends or I was his girlfriend or something.

"You know, I used to get beat up by black kids all the time," he told me. I tried to tune him out, but it was kinda hard to do when he was two inches from my face. "They made fun of me because I was chunky. A group of them beat me up and dunked my face in the toilet."

He went on and on about how much he couldn't stand black people. How he used to have a girlfriend after his wife left him. How people had done all this horrible sexual stuff to him when he was young. How much he loved to watch porn whenever he got the chance. How he loved looking at blonde girls.

"I wish I had gotten to that little JonBenet Ramsey first," he said. "If some other bastard didn't get her first, that coulda been me." He smiled, and I wanted to punch him right in the teeth.

Another time he made the same kind of nasty comment about Elizabeth Smart, who was abducted just two months before I was, in the summer of 2002. "I know—I'm a sick man," he said. "I hate the way I am."

"Then why are you doing what you're doing?" My voice was shaky. "Just because somebody did something bad to you doesn't mean you can turn around and do bad things to other people."

He was quiet for a minute before he said, "I can't help myself. I have to hurt you."

"You are sick," I said. Seeing him frown, I added, "But there's help for people like you. Why don't you let me go so you can get some help? I won't tell anyone you took me. Just let me go, and we can forget this ever happened."

For a minute he seemed to be thinking about it. I held my breath. Then he frowned, and my heart sank. "I can't do that," he said, shaking his head. "You're gonna have to stay with me for a while."

I began to cry. "All I want to do is go back to Joey!" I begged him. "He's only two years old—I know he's missing me! Can't you just let me go?"

He paused for a long time, and I hoped against hope that he had a shred of humanity in him. "Don't cry," he said finally. "You're not supposed to be sad. I want you to be happy here with me. We're supposed to be a family."

I couldn't believe what I was hearing. This warped dude had kidnapped me, beat me, and raped me every day—and he expected us to be a *family?* I knew he wasn't just sick; he was a total psycho. He was living in his own fantasy world— and I had to find a way out of it. I tried to pretend like I was falling asleep so he would leave the room. He passed out with his heavy, hairy arm draped across my middle and started snoring. Slowly I tried to wiggle the chains to see if they'd give a little, but every time I moved an inch, he'd grunt and grip me tighter.

Finally, in the afternoon, he woke up. "Don't even think about screaming, or I will come up here and shoot you," he said as he walked out.

*Oh my God—he has a gun.* He slammed the door, and after a while I heard his truck leaving.

I sat up on the mattress and looked at the two locks on my chains. One was a combination lock, and the other one was a padlock that opened with a key. I'd tried many times before in the basement, but I thought maybe today I could get the combination lock open. I twisted the knob, trying different combinations of numbers: Joey's birthday. My birthday. Random numbers. I pulled real hard on the handle each time, but nothing worked.

After another hour of fiddling with the lock, I looked out the window to see the sun going down. That's when I started praying—and I prayed harder than I have ever prayed in my life. "God, please help me to get away from this nut," I said with tears running down my face. "I really need you to get me out of this house. I need to see my son again. Please, God. Please." I said that same prayer over and over again until the sky went pitch-black, and finally I fell asleep.

In the morning the sound of the dude's boots on the stairs woke me up. When he opened the door, he was holding a hammer and some nails. He pulled a sandwich in a yellow wrapper from his pocket. Then he handed me the sandwich and stomped back downstairs. I gobbled it down, dreading whatever he was planning next. What was he going to do with the tools? Did he have some new torture planned for me? I heard him coming back up the stairs, more slowly this time. He grunted and pushed into the room holding a stack of boards, which he dumped onto the floor. Something was making his back pocket bulge. Suddenly I was covered in cold sweat.

"What are those for?" I asked in a wobbly voice. *Is he building a coffin for me? Is that bulge in his back pocket the gun?*

He smiled a sick smile at me and reached his hand back to his pocket. Right then and there, I knew I was going to die.

*Please God, let Joey know that I loved him. Let him know I never stopped thinking about him. That he was the light of my life . . .*

The dude pulled something out of his pocket; I saw the flash of gunmetal in his hand. *Oh my God, here it comes . . . God, I'm going to die . . .*

He pointed the gun right at me. It took a full minute before I realized that it was a cordless drill.

"You're gonna help me board up all these windows," he said. "Pick up one of them boards and hold it so I can make some holes."

I was weak with relief that he wasn't planning to shoot me. He unlocked the chains, then made me help him board up all the windows on the second floor. There was the pink room where he'd first hung me up, and the white room through a connecting door. There were also two other rooms across the hall: another pink room, and a blue one. In each room he forced me to hold up the boards while he drilled holes in them and hammered them in place with long nails. After it was all done, he moved me into the blue room. With a sinking heart I realized he was building a prison—and he was making extra sure I could never get out of it.

I HAD BEEN locked up in the blue room for couple of weeks when I started talking to Joey again. By my count, I was pretty sure it was at least Thanksgiving, and maybe even early December; that meant Christmas was just around the corner. It didn't seem like the bastard was anywhere close to letting me go like he said he would; as a matter of fact, he had never brought that up again. Instead, one day he told me, "I'll let you go after I get two other girls." He checked my chains and went down the stairs.

*Oh my God,* I thought. *He's planning to kidnap someone else!* I hoped he'd get caught in the act, arrested, and locked away. But then the thought occurred to me: Would anyone ever find me if he got put in prison? Would I die here, wasting away in this upstairs bedroom? Would they find me a year from now, a decaying carcass wrapped in chains? Would they ever figure out who I was? I wondered what he'd done with my bag. Would they even be able to identify my body? I was sure he'd gotten rid of my wallet with my ID and the baby picture of Joey in it.

I tried to get myself together. Because it didn't look like I was going to be set free anytime soon, I tried to do whatever I could to fill the hours. I thought about the day I saw Joey take his first steps. At eleven months, he'd been toddling around the house holding onto the edges of tables and chairs, and I'd walk him around and around holding onto his hand. He'd sit on the floor and bounce on his bottom, like he was practicing standing up. One afternoon I was sitting in a chair as he was bouncing like that.

"Come on, Joey! You can do it! Come to Mommy!" I called out.

With a big smile, his two little front teeth showing, he stood up and took a step toward me. Then another. I held my breath, not wanting to say anything that would distract him. He took two more fast steps, and then he sat down on his bottom, padded by his diaper. His little face looked surprised, then he burst into tears.

I scooped him up into my arms. "You did it, huggy bear! You took your first steps!" I said as I hugged him. He stopped crying and looked at me, his eyelashes wet from his tears. His big brown eyes were such a beautiful color.

"That was great!" I said. "You know what, you're gonna be an incredible soccer player! I'm gonna get you a soccer ball this year!"

Suddenly a shadow filled the doorway. The dude walked in, and I realized I'd been speaking out loud. "Who the hell are you talking to?" he shouted.

"Joey," I said. "I talk to him every day."

He looked at me like I was out of my mind. "You're a crazy little slut, aren't you?" he said. *If that isn't the pot calling the kettle black,* I thought. "Stop talking to people who ain't there," he added.

That's when an idea popped into my head. "Well, if you finally got me the puppy you promised me," I told him, "I wouldn't have to talk to Joey."

Every chance I got I reminded him that he'd brought me to his house the first time because he said he had a puppy. I thought that at least if I had a dog, it would help me pass the endless hours I spent chained up with just the four blue walls for company, the windows boarded up so I couldn't even see a bird flying or clouds drifting past outside.

My little trick worked—in two ways. A few days later the dude put a small, old radio on the mattress and plugged it into the wall. "I know you get bored," he said, "so you can listen to this thing sometimes. But don't play it too loud, or I'll take it away. And no listening to music from niggers."

I was almost too excited to pay attention to his stupid rules—I had my own radio! Do you know what it's like not to hear music for months? Or human voices, other than the dude's—and he didn't really count as a human being. I turned the volume real low and went through every station. I finally got it on the one that was always my favorite—97.1 FM. The only thing I wished was that I could dance around the room for exercise. But the chains were too tight for that.

It was even hard to use the bucket that was right next to the mattress.

Not even a whole week after that I got another huge surprise. The dude showed up in my room with a cardboard box. In it I heard whimpering. It was a puppy!

"Here. He's yours," he told me as he set the box on the floor next to the mattress. He actually seemed happy when he gave it to me—like he was giving a dog to his daughter or something. A little brown and white pit bull jumped up onto the side of the cardboard. "Just make sure you only let him take a dump inside the box," he said.

I fell for that little dog from his very first yip. I named him Lobo, because he was low to the ground. He was a little shorty like me! I taught him how to go potty right in the box. Whenever the dude came upstairs, he brought a plastic bag with him so he could scoop up some of Lobo's poop and take it outside. A lot of times he took Lobo out to let him poop and then left him chained in the yard while he came back in and raped me. To be honest, he cleaned up after the dog more than he cleaned up after me—he hardly ever even took out my bucket! The room smelled like a cesspool. But once I had the puppy, I didn't notice it as much. Every night Lobo curled up right beside me and we fell asleep together.

I loved that dog with all of my heart. Having him in that room with me brightened up my days so much. He'd snuffle in my ear and lick my face in the morning when he woke up, and I'd put him in his box so he could pee. Then I'd take him out and hold him in my lap, rubbing his silky ears as he stared up at me, like he adored me. I'd tell Lobo everything we were going to do that day; it didn't matter to him if we never actually got to do any of it.

"Hey, Lobo," I'd whisper, not wanting the dude to hear me from downstairs. "We're finally gonna go for a walk today! I'm going to take you out for a nice stroll around the neighborhood. I'll put you on a leash so you don't chase any squirrels or get hit by a car. I'm going to teach you how to walk proper on a leash. Then we'll stop by my cousin Lisa's …"

Here, I paused. Was my family looking for me, or had they given up? What were Eddie and Freddie doing now? They had moved out of my mother's house by the time I left; I wondered if they were still even in Cleveland at this point. Wherever they were, I felt sure they must miss me. Lobo gazed up into my face, looking worried. I swear that dog knew everything I was feeling. I could tell he felt sad when I cried and happy when I smiled.

"It's okay, boy," I said, stroking his head. "I'm all right. We'll go for that walk a little bit later," I said as I heard footsteps stomping up the steps. "You'd better go back in now," I said, quickly lifting him and putting him in the box.

ONE EVENING A few months after I got Lobo, the dude came shuffling upstairs. The minute he came through the door, I knew he was drunk. He was slurring his words and falling all over the place, and he reeked of rum. He didn't take Lobo downstairs before he tried to get on top of me.

"Bring your ass over here," he told me. Before I could move, he grabbed me by my hair and dragged me, still in chains, to the edge of the mattress. "You're gonna do everything I tell you to do tonight."

When Lobo saw the dude roughing me up, he went crazy, barking.

"Shut up, you stupid dog!" he yelled.

But Lobo kept right on barking. The dude slapped me in the face and yelled, "Make him stop!" My cheek felt like somebody had just set it on fire. A second later Lobo ran at his leg and tried to bite him, but before he could sink in his teeth, the dude picked him up.

Without blinking an eye, he used his big hands to break the dog's neck. Lobo let out one last yelp, and then his body went limp. The dude threw my puppy's broken body right onto the mattress.

"You killed my baby!" I screamed. "Get out! Get out right now!" I beat at him with my fists. I didn't care what he did to me now.

He did get out—but he took me and Lobo's body with him. He unchained me from the bed and dumped the dog in his cardboard box. Then, carrying the box in one arm, he dragged me downstairs. At the back door he warned me, "I dare you to move from this spot." Then he walked outside and threw Lobo's body over the back fence. I knew he would knock the piss out of me later, but I sobbed and screamed as loud as I could from the open door, and not just because my little sweetie was gone. I also wanted someone—*anyone*—to hear me. But apparently no one did.

# 12

## The Backyard

WITHOUT MY LITTLE LOBO, the days went back to endless hours of boredom. I still had the radio, but I missed my puppy with all my heart. I talked to Joey every day, and sometimes I talked to Lobo too.

"You're a good boy," I'd tell him. I'd shut my eyes and pretend I was holding him in my lap, stroking his soft puppy fur. "You're my sweet little dog. We'll always be together." Sometimes I wondered if I'd join him in death, my neck broken too by the insane man who kept me captive.

One afternoon the dude came upstairs and unchained me. "I'm going to let you sit on the back porch," he said.

That was the crazy thing about him: you could never tell what he was going to do next. Some days he would bring you a radio and a puppy; other days he was a violent storm—a raging drunk who raped you and then snapped your puppy's neck. The man who'd abused me for years in my parents' house never did anything close to nice, but at least I always knew what to expect from that prick. But this dude was so twisted that it was hard to figure out how to deal with him. Even when it seemed like he might be doing something that was good for me—such as letting me go outdoors—I knew I couldn't trust him.

But I *did* want to fool him into thinking he could trust *me.* I had been working on that for a while. Sometimes he would slam the back door like he was going to work, and then he would come back fifteen minutes later to see if I had moved. He tried to be real quiet when he came up the stairs so I wouldn't know he was spying on me. But not only could I hear him, I knew he hadn't left in the first place. He probably didn't realize I could hear the van coming in and out of the driveway. When he sneaked upstairs and peeked in my room, I just laid on the mattress like I was asleep and played along with him. I could feel him staring at me through a crack in the door.

I don't know why he thought I could get out. *Seriously, dude. I'm chained up with two huge locks. Where in the hell do you think I'm going?* I figured it was just more of his craziness. And I'm pretty sure he was trying to scare me by testing me. He was playing a mental game, wanting me to think that if I ever tried to escape, he would catch me. One time, when he brought me down to the kitchen with him, I noticed he left the back door open just a little bit, I think on purpose. I didn't try to go out the door. I knew I wouldn't have made it off the porch before he would have grabbed me by the back of my hair. So I just sat at the kitchen table and pretended like I didn't see that the door was open.

On the afternoon he took me out to the porch, he threw a large green T-shirt and some gray sweatpants onto the bed. "Put these on," he said. The green shirt was covered with oil stains. The pants were way too long for me. Both of the clothes smelled like him—horrible. But believe it or not, they still smelled less foul than I did! While he was standing there, I took off my own T-shirt and put on his green one. I kept on my butterfly underwear and put the sweatpants over them.

"Follow me," he said. We went downstairs and stopped in the kitchen. He started searching for something. That's when I got my first real good look at where the dude must have slept. Not too far from the kitchen I saw a tiny room. It didn't have a door, so I could see right inside. There was a TV with a VCR and a queen-size bed. A guitar was in the corner. *That must be the one he plays in his band,* I thought. That's about all that could fit in there. It was really just a cubbyhole without a door.

From a kitchen drawer he pulled out a wig and some huge sunglasses. The wig had long brown hair that was matted up and ugly. He shoved the glasses onto my face and put the wig on my head. The strands of fake hair were bristly; they felt like little pieces of wire hitting the back of my neck. The sunglasses were so big that they covered most of my face. I wondered if anyone else had worn the wig, and who it belonged to.

He opened another drawer and got something out of it. When he turned around, I saw what he was holding: a handgun.

"If you try anything stupid when we get outside, I'll shoot you," he said. He waved the gun in front of my face and let out the little evil laugh that I'd gotten used to. "Don't think I won't kill you, because I will. This thing is loaded." If he was trying to scare the bejesus outta me, it worked. I was quaking behind the sunglasses. He put the gun in the back pocket of his jeans.

Then he pushed me out the back door and onto the porch. *Aah, fresh air! Sunshine!* It was the first time in over three months that I'd been outdoors. It was pretty chilly that day, and I folded my arms around myself to get a little warmer. Then I took a look around the yard. It was just as junky as it had been the first day I got there back in August. There were rusty chains like the ones in the basement lying around everywhere.

Maxine, the dog, was chained to a pole. She barked a little when we came out, and then she settled down. I saw tools and car parts, old oily rags, and paper trash all over the place. It looked like he was building something on the porch. There was a long piece of wood and an electric saw on a table.

"I'm going to saw this wood in half, and you're going to help me," he said.

I held up one side of the board, and he cut through it with the noisy saw. The whole time he kept giving me this wicked grin, like he really wanted to cut *me* in half. The dust from the wood got underneath the big sunglasses and up into my nose. I started to cough and sneeze a little. "Go sit down over there," he told me. He pointed to a dirty folding chair. I walked over and sat down. He didn't take his eyeballs off of me the whole time.

In the backyard next door I suddenly saw an old white guy, but it wasn't the same guy who waved to me the day I came into the house. He looked at both of us, but he didn't say anything. I wanted to shout, "Please help me! Can't you see I'm in trouble? Call the police!" But I was too afraid of what the nutjob would do.

When I looked back at the dude, he was staring me right in the face. He ran his hand over the gun in his back pocket, like he was reminding me, "If you make a move, I will shoot you." I figured he was just crazy enough to do it, so I sat very still. When I saw the neighbor go back inside, I was hoping, *Maybe he knows this looks weird. Maybe he went to call the cops!* But if he did call, the cops never showed up. How could a man see a girl dressed in such a weird way, with no coat on a cold day, and not think something was off? I just didn't understand that; it made me furious. It still does.

We stayed outside for about a half hour before he took me back to my blue prison. He made me give him back all of my clothes—not just the green shirt and sweats, but my T-shirt and underwear too. So now I was totally naked when he chained me up.

"I'm cold," I told him. "I need those clothes!"

He shrugged. "You're gonna stay naked as long as I want you to stay naked," he said. Then he walked out.

I lay on the mattress with my teeth chattering. He didn't give me any clothes for the next four months.

Looking back on it now, it seems like it was kind of stupid for him to take me outside—what if someone in the neighborhood thought I looked suspicious with the wig and glasses on? But then again, he already knew no one was looking for me. Just about every day he reminded me that he did not see one single thing on TV or any fliers in the neighborhood about my disappearance.

"You're a nobody," he always told me. I didn't say anything back, but I wondered if he was lying. Surely someone in my family had notified the police that I was missing? I hoped to God that was true.

At least one sort of good thing came out of my afternoon on the back porch. Once again I had showed the dude that he could "trust" me to not try and get away. I figured if I kept doing that long enough, maybe he would relax and let down his guard. And then I could make a break for it.

A few weeks later it was Christmas. I knew that because I'd been listening to the radio. All that day I sat on the bed and cried. My eyes stung because I had rubbed them so hard. He showed up in my room with a white cake that had red and green sprinkles all over it. It looked like it came from the supermarket. "Here. Merry Christmas," he said. He set the cake on the floor and stared at me from head to toe, like I was a piece of meat. My body was blue from the cold. "Now you know what you need to do if you want some of that," he said. I didn't even look at him.

While the dude raped me that night, I thought about everything I had missed. *September. October. November. December.* The year had gone away. My desire to live had almost gone with it. I felt so alone, depressed, and scared. *How could I still be here?* Only one thing kept me breathing—the thought of Joey.

I wondered how my huggy bear was spending his Christmas. *Who are his new foster parents? Is he as happy today as he was on the Christmas when we got up so early and sang together? Does he wonder where his mother has gone? Does he miss me every day?* I didn't have any answers. All I had was a monster on top of me—and a grocery store cake that I refused to touch.

# 13

## TV & a Shower

DECEMBER WAS COLD—BUT in January I almost froze. Every time he came up to my room, I pleaded for him to give me something to wear. But he wouldn't give me anything.

"You're not here to stay warm," he told me. "You're only here for one thing."

By the end of February I swear to you that I couldn't even feel my lips and toes anymore. I begged him again for a shirt, some gloves, a hat, some socks or sweats—*something*. He finally threw me a tiny piece of cotton material. It was like a torn piece of sheet. It was hardly big enough to cover my little body, but it was better than nothing.

There was a radiator near my bed, but whenever I stretched over to feel it, it was barely warm. The whole house was freezing. On a lot of days I could see my breath. All I could do was try to bury my body underneath my small pillow—I tried to turn that thing into an igloo. The only time I got warm is when the dude put himself inside of me, but honestly, I think I would have preferred to freeze to death.

Around March he came into my room with a small color TV. "I know you get bored," he said. He set the TV on a little shelf next to the mattress. With my chains on, I could just reach it. "You won't have this for very long, so don't get used to it," he said. "And don't let me catch you watching any niggers either."

He plugged it in and put the volume on low. It seemed weird to me that he would give a girl he kidnapped a TV, but nothing he did made sense. I thought, *Really? Now you care about me being bored, with all the disgusting stuff you do to me, and not giving me a shred of clothes for the past two months? And on top of that, you're worried about me looking at black people?*

That TV changed my life. All of a sudden I had a way to find out what was going on outside of that creepy house, the things that I couldn't learn from just the radio. Not only could I hear the news; I could *see* the news and what was happening around the country. I could watch some TV shows instead of just hearing music. It really helped to pass the time—and all I had was time.

Not a day went by that I didn't dream about Joey and wonder what he was doing. *Did he go to the store today? Did he have a nightmare that I wasn't there for? Did he play at the park? Does he have a dog now? Was his name changed? Are things happening in the world that would affect him?* So when the dude showed up with a TV, I kinda went nuts on the inside, but on the outside I tried to act like I didn't care.

Although he told me not to turn to the news or watch black people, sometimes I did anyway. One huge news item happened in the middle of March, when Elizabeth Smart was found. I was so glad she was alive and got to go back home. It gave me hope that maybe I'd be discovered and set free too.

I also caught up on a lot of other stuff: Michael Jackson had held his baby over a balcony the year before (*Oh my God*). The Anaheim Angels had beat the San Francisco Giants to win the World Series (for some reason, I loved baseball ... I always wished I was tall enough to play). I found out that Kelly Clarkson had won the first season of *American Idol,* but I couldn't catch every episode of the second season because there were so many black contestants and I knew the dude might walk in and see them. I later heard that Reuben Stoddard won. I could have told you *that* would happen ... that guy could *sing!*

My favorite show was *Everybody Loves Raymond.* It made me laugh so hard that I almost had to pee on myself, but it also sometimes made me sad. In some of the episodes Raymond took his family out for fun. They would go to the movies or to the park. One time he even had a romantic dinner with his wife. Things like that made me cry because I didn't have that—and I knew I might *never* have that. It was like the whole world was just moving on and living their lives while I was stuck in a hellhole.

Even when the dude came up to my room at night, he let me keep the TV on, for whatever reason. When I heard his boots hitting the stairs, I'd hurry up and change the station to make sure there was no black person on the screen. Sometimes while he did his thing to me, I would turn my head to the side and try to catch the latest episode of *Everybody Loves Raymond.* Every time something funny happened I could hear the audience cracking up. It was kind of weird to hear all that laughing while a man was on top of me—because on the inside I was crying so hard.

NOT LONG AFTER I received the TV I got another surprise—a shower.

"You stink," the dude said to me one morning. *No shit, Sherlock.* After almost eight months with no shower, I was pretty gross. My white skin looked brown. I had smudges of dried blood, dirt, and pee all over me. My legs were so hairy that they looked like a man's. And I never got used to the way I smelled. It was so bad that it sometimes made me gag.

"I'm going to take you down to the bathroom so you can wash up," he said. *Is this some kind of mean trick? Or another test? Or is he really going to let me clean myself up?* I had no idea. He unchained me and I followed him out. Going down the stairs made me a little dizzy after so long stuck in the blue room, so I took each step slowly.

The bathroom was on the main floor. I had never been inside it. He opened the door and said, "I'll wait for you out here." He handed me a tiny sliver of soap. "Make it quick," he said as I walked through the door.

The bathroom was a total wreck. The toilet was covered with flaking brown dirt. Spider webs were in every corner. All kinds of trash covered the floor. There was mildew on the walls. I put down the toilet seat and sat on it. For once, I wanted to use a bathroom like a normal person instead of like a wild animal. As my pee hit the water, I could feel the whole toilet bowl rocking back and forth; it wasn't totally bolted down to the ground. There wasn't any toilet paper. I had just one thought: *How the hell does anyone live like this?*

I looked at myself in the mirror above the sink. I looked hideous; I couldn't believe it was me. My brown hair was now shoulder-length and was standing up in every direction. It was so full of semen that it was hard as a rock. My eyes were bloodshot from the months of constant tears. My face was pale because I hardly ever saw sunlight. There were deep purple-and-yellow bruises on both sides of my face from all the times he'd socked me in the head. I started to cry. *Is this really happening? Will I spend the rest of my life here?* I wondered. Even though I had been in the house for about eight months, I still felt like I was trapped in some kind of horror movie. But seeing my bruised face told me just how real this all was. Looking at my hair, I decided at least I could try to do something about that.

The dude pounded his fist on the door and shouted, "Hurry up in there!" I stepped inside the tub. It was filthy and had a ring of black dirt all the way around it. I turned on the hot water. Even after it ran for a minute, only cold water came out. So I gritted my teeth and stepped right under it. *Oh God*—it was ice cold. I scrubbed myself all over with the little sliver of soap. The water coming off of me was black.

"What the hell are you doing in there?" the dude yelled.

I got out of the shower real quick and poked my head out the door. "Can I have some scissors?" I asked.

He gave me a weird look that made me think he wasn't going to give me any. But then he stepped away and came back with a small pair. He handed them to me, and for whatever reason, he didn't ask me why I needed them. "You've got five minutes to get your ass outta there," he said.

I hurried back into the shower and held the scissors up to my head. Of course they were dull, so they wouldn't have worked as a weapon. I had to squeeze them really hard to make them cut through my matted hair. *Snip. Snip. Snip.* My hair was so stiff that to wash it, I had to cut it real short, all the way up to my ears. My hair ran into the drain. The tub was so nasty that I could barely tell which part was my hair and which part was the ring of dirt. I tried to cut some of the itchy hair off my legs, too, but the scissors weren't sharp enough.

I didn't have any way to dry myself, so I just did my best to shake off some water and wipe the rest with my hands. I opened the bathroom door to find the dude still standing there. He snatched the scissors out of my hand.

"You cut your hair off." He seemed surprised. I didn't answer him. "Let's go," he said. He then shoved me into his tiny room that was on the main floor. "Get up there," he said. He pointed to the top of the bed, where he had put in chains and locks like the ones he had upstairs. He locked me in, and I laid there while he watched some wacky show on cable TV about people who have strange fetishes. Then he watched a porn video. Then another one. Then another one. That's when he pulled me over to his side of the bed and started playing with my breasts. Then while he was raping me, he forced me to say certain things to him.

"Tell me you're enjoying it!" he shouted. I wouldn't say it, so he slapped me in the head. My hair was still wet from the shower. "Tell me my dick is good! Call me Big Daddy!"

For a long time I would not cooperate—and he kept right on hitting me. I started to see that the whole thing was going to last a lot longer if I ignored him, so I ended up saying what he told me to say. But every time one of those sick words came out of my mouth, I hated myself for giving in.

# 14

## The Second Girl

"Yesterday on april 21, sixteen-year-old Amanda Berry was reported missing." When I heard a TV news reporter say those words, I got up and leaned over to the TV to turn up the volume a little bit. "The girl was last seen leaving her job at Burger King on Lorain Avenue and West 110th Street in Cleveland."

*That's close to here,* I thought. A picture of a blonde girl flashed up on the screen. I recognized her picture! *That's the girl who used to be in my art class!* I realized. She was a lot younger than me, but I was so far behind in school that we ended up in some of the same classes.

Right away I had a sick feeling in my gut that the dude had snatched Amanda. He was always saying, "As soon as I get two more girls, I will let you go."

Amanda seemed like the type of girl he claimed to like: young and blonde. He was always talking about how much he wanted to have sex with blondes like Britney Spears and Christina Aguilera. Plus, I knew exactly where that Burger King was; it wasn't far from his house, and he was always going to fast food restaurants. Putting together all the clues, I was sure he did it. A couple of days after I saw the report on TV, I started listening closely for new noises in the house. But I didn't hear anything, and I started thinking that maybe I was wrong.

But then three or four weeks later something happened. The dude started blasting music all the time, more than he usually did. And it sounded like it was coming from the basement, not from his room. *He must have Amanda locked in the basement—the same way he did me,* I thought. I figured he didn't want me to hear her screaming her head off. Whatever was happening, I knew it couldn't be good.

One afternoon the dude came up to my room and sat on the mattress. "I want to introduce you to someone I brung into the house," he said.

I was quiet for a while before I said anything. I was so furious at him for taking another girl. He couldn't be satisfied with ruining only my life—he had to ruin another person's too? I was so angry, I decided to confront him with it, no matter how mad he got.

"You don't have to tell me her name—I already know it's Amanda." He stared at me like he was surprised.

"How do you know?" he asked.

"I saw her on TV. I used to go to school with her. I'm not retarded. I know what you did."

He got real quiet. "It's not Amanda," he finally said. Then he got up and left.

The next day he moved me from the blue room back to the pink room. The windows were still boarded up from the day he made me help him close the place down. He had attached chains to the bed and walls in there too, which he used to tie me down. There was trash all over the place—half-eaten pizzas still in the boxes, spoiled sandwiches, Chinese food dried up in the bottom of white take-out containers. It looked like he'd been eating up there every day and throwing his leftovers on the floor. It was a stinky mess.

After I was locked in, he took away my TV. "I'm going to give this to Amanda," he said. *Is he going down to the basement with it—or is he bringing Amanda upstairs to a room?* I had no clue. But I did hear him making a lot of noise in the connecting white room. *Maybe he put the TV there*, I thought.

Later on that same day he came back to my room with another TV, an old, tiny black-and-white one with bunny ears. "You're gonna use this TV from now on," he told me. He put it next to my bed. When I tried to turn up the volume, even all the way, I could barely hear anything. "This doesn't work," I said. He shrugged and left the room.

The next day he took me out of the chains and then left the room again. A minute later he came back in the room with Amanda. I recognized her from art class and TV. As soon as I saw her, I quickly pulled the little sheet over the middle of my naked body.

"She got the same thing you got!" he said when he saw me trying to cover up. "This is my brother's girlfriend," he said. I couldn't believe he'd try to tell me such a stupid lie. I just stared at him.

Amanda was not the smiling girl I remembered from art class. She didn't speak or act like she recognized me. We just stared at each other. Understandably, she looked frightened and kind of out of it. Her shoulder-length blonde hair was pulled back in a ponytail. She was wearing gray pajamas that were too big for her. I could tell the PJs were men's because there was an opening in the front of the pants. She looked all around the room at the ankle-deep garbage, the boarded-up windows. I imagined that she was in shock at what a disaster the house was and by the fact that she was now a prisoner here. Then he left with her. The whole meeting lasted for less than a minute.

The next day the dude came in and unchained me. "Let's go," he said. He led me over to the white room. Amanda was sitting there on the mattress. She barely looked up at either one of us when we came in. *I guess this is where he's going to keep her,* I thought. I felt so sorry for this young girl and what she was going to have to go through. I just hoped her ordeal wouldn't be as bad as mine had been.

At first I thought Amanda didn't have chains, but then she moved her leg, and I saw a chain around her ankle. She had clothes on—sweats and a T-shirt, as I recall. *I wonder why she gets to wear clothes?* I thought. The color TV he'd taken out of my room was on a dresser near her bed. When I first saw her that afternoon, again I tried to cover my naked body with my arms and hands. I was so embarrassed, but there was nothing I could do about it. The dude walked back to the other room, and I could hear him searching for something in the closet.

"I know who you are from school," I said to her. "You were in my art class." She looked right into my face. "I went to John Marshall High," she finally said in a quiet voice.

I nodded. "So did I." I still wasn't sure if she remembered me; I figured she probably didn't because I always sat at the back of the class. I tried to think of something I could say that would make her feel less scared.

"How old are you?" she asked.

"I'm twenty-two." Just a few weeks before, a radio DJ had said that it was April 23—my birthday.

Amanda raised her eyebrows. "You look like you're thirteen. When did—"

Right then the dude came back in. He handed me a white, extra-long men's T-shirt. I quickly slipped it over my head.

I didn't know it then, but I wouldn't have the chance to talk to Amanda again for a long time—for *months*. On some days I could hear him unchain her and take her down to his room on the main floor; it broke my heart to think about what he was probably doing to her down there. On days while the dude was at work I could hear Amanda's TV. If I happened to see something about her kidnapping on my TV, I would turn up the volume as loud as it would go. Even though the volume was pretty much broken, I hoped she would hear it and realize she should turn on her TV and watch. She must have been miserable, so I wanted her to know that people were still looking for her. I might have felt alone and forgotten, but I didn't want someone else to go through that too.

A few times after Amanda got to the house, the dude brought us both down to the kitchen. I have no clue why. We didn't really have a chance to talk to each other; we just said "hi" and gave each other a very quick hug. If he stepped out of the room for a second, I would quietly tell her, "Everything is going to be okay. One day we'll get home." Her eyes were red like she had been crying.

I could tell the dude didn't want us to spend time together. Even when he did have us in the same room, he made sure it was for less than five minutes. There were so many questions I wanted to ask Amanda: How did he get you into the house?

Did he keep you in the basement with that helmet on when you first got here, and is that why I didn't see you for a while? What kind of stuff does he do to you when he comes to your room? Are you as scared shitless as I am? And most important of all: Do you think we have a chance of getting out of this torture chamber?

That spring the dude never admitted to me that Amanda wasn't his brother's girlfriend. I don't know why he told me that stupid lie after I told him I knew it was Amanda, and that I had gone to school with her. One night, when the dude took me down to his cubbyhole room, he turned on his cable TV. Amanda's mother was on the news pleading for people to help find her daughter.

He laughed. "I'm smarter than those stupid cops," he said. "You see that?" he added, pointing up in the direction of the stairs. "At least someone is looking for her. But who's looking for you? Not a soul. That's because you don't mean nothin' to nobody. I can keep you in here forever and nobody will miss you."

I would have cried, but when you've been locked away for nearly a year, you sort of run out of tears. I wondered if anyone was looking for me, why no one from my family was on TV. Even though I'd been missing for a while, you'd think that Amanda's disappearance would trigger questions about whether the same person had kidnapped me—that is, if anyone had ever made a big deal about me being gone in the first place.

# 15

# Pregnant

Not too long after Amanda was brought into the house, I woke up feeling sick—wicked sick. I tried to eat a little bit of some leftover pizza the dude dropped off, but I threw it up. My breasts were very sore. I started throwing up all the food he gave me. I knew I was pregnant; I felt the exact same way I did when I was first pregnant with Joey.

The dude didn't figure it out right away. My room was so disgusting that he probably didn't even notice my vomit on the floor. In fact, I tried to hide the pregnancy from him because I didn't know what he would do if he found out. No matter how sick I felt when he came in the room, I acted like I was fine. I know it might sound crazy, but in my weakened and disoriented state of mind, I thought I did want to have another child. I missed my son so much that my whole body ached. And I didn't even have my little Lobo anymore. At least I could have something that was all mine, a baby growing inside of me, even though the baby's father was the Devil himself.

For the next few weeks after he'd brought Amanda to the house he seemed to come to my room a lot more often— in the morning before work and then two or three times at night.

"She don't want to do it," he told me, "so you're gonna have to do it."

As much as I hated it when he came to my room, I was happy to hear that Amanda was fending him off. "I don't want to force her do things and then make her cry," he added.

I thought, *But you're okay with making* me *cry?* I wondered why he seemed to be treating her different from how he was treating me. Why she got the better TV. Why he made me do the most sick sexual acts with him and tell me it was because she didn't feel like it. I figured it was because he had an obsession with blondes. But I didn't blame Amanda for the way the dude treated either one of us. He was the psycho bastard who had us both chained up; the whole situation was a result of his twisted mind.

One night he started biting and sucking my nipples real hard. He was always telling me how he had a thing for girls with big boobs; I'm pretty sure that was one of the main reasons he chose to kidnap me.

All of a sudden he stopped. "What's this?" he said. A little bit of white liquid had leaked from my nipple. He wiped it off with his hand and looked at it. It was breast milk.

"You must be pregnant, you little slut!" he shouted. Right away he got off of me. "There's no way in hell you're having a baby in this house!" he shouted. He slammed the door and pounded down the stairs.

The bastard started trying to starve me so I'd lose the baby. He still came into my room to get his sex every morning and night, but he never brought any food. One night after he'd been starving me for a couple of weeks, he came into my room holding a huge barbell.

Holy crap, I thought. What is he going to do with that?

My whole body shook with terror as he walked over to my bed. He put down the barbell, grabbed my foot, and pulled me over the edge of the mattress.

"It's time to get rid of this little problem," he said. "Stand up, bitch."

"No!" I shouted. "Keep away from me!" But he yanked me up and onto the floor. The chains cut into my neck as he pulled me upright.

As soon as he picked up the barbell again, I started screaming my head off. "No, no, no!" I yelled. "Stop it! Please don't kill my baby!" I tried to get away from him by getting back onto the bed, but he grabbed my hair. And then with one hard swing—*Bam!*—he punched me in the stomach with the barbell.

I screamed bloody murder and fell to my knees. In horrible pain, I hugged my arms across my stomach. "I hate you!" I yelled. I was sobbing so hysterically that the whole neighborhood should have heard me. "Get out!" I screamed. "I hate you!"

He gave me an evil look. "Tomorrow it had better be gone," he said, before he left the room.

I cried into my pillow for hours. My stomach felt like someone had just driven over it with an eight-wheel truck. Blood was rushing from between my legs, all over the place. I tried to use my sheet to stop the bleeding, but it was coming out too fast. I was in so much pain that I passed out. When I woke up, I think it was the middle of the night. I lay on my mattress in the pitch-black and sobbed uncontrollably. I felt like I wanted to die. The only thing that kept me breathing was that someday I wanted see my Joey again.

Just as the sun was coming up I started having horrible cramps. Minutes later I felt something slide out of me. It was the most god-awful thing I had ever lived through. The dude came upstairs before work and saw the big mess on my mattress.

"You aborted my child!" he yelled. He slapped me so hard in the face that I saw stars. "That'll teach you not to kill my baby, you slut!"

All I could do was lay there and stare into space.

THE REST OF 2003 and the first part of 2004 went by very, very, very slowly. Every week was exactly the same as the one before it: five straight mornings of McDonald's breakfast, followed by rape. Hours of boredom from morning until afternoon. More of me being violated at night after the dude came home. Loud Spanish music over the weekends. I thought I would lose my mind.

I knew Amanda was still in the house because sometimes I could hear her moving around (her steps sounded much lighter on the staircase than his elephant steps), but she and I still rarely saw each other. A couple of times I took a chance and tried to yell something to her after I knew the dude had gone out, but I never got an answer. She probably couldn't hear me over the noise of her TV from wherever he had her chained up.

I didn't get to go downstairs very often, but once, when he took me to the kitchen, I noticed that he'd put up alarms all over the place—by the windows and above the doors. There were also little mirrors everywhere, like rearview mirrors he had put up so he could see what was happening from every direction. Seeing all of that really made me feel like there was no hope of escaping.

At this point I stopped thinking too much about how I could break out of the house. It seemed like everything I'd thought of—trying to wiggle my hands out of the chains, trying to get away from him while he raped me—had failed. He kept me chained up almost all of the time, and when I was unlocked, he was always with me and watching me closely. I couldn't work the padlocks loose. And the few times he took me on the back porch, he threatened me with his gun. I don't think of myself as a quitter, but after you've wracked your brain for every possible way to escape and nothing works out, you start to give up a little. I guess I just started feeling hopeless. I was also terrified that if he caught me, he would blow my brains out. And what good would I ever be to Joey if I got myself killed by this bastard? None!

One afternoon in the spring of 2004 I heard another news report that freaked me out. On April 2 fourteen-year-old Gina DeJesus had gone missing from the same area where Amanda and I had been kidnapped. Just like I had recognized Amanda, I also knew who Gina was—her older sister, Mayra, went to my school. In my heart I was pretty sure the dude had kidnapped her. That evening I prayed so hard that I was wrong.

Later that same night I heard a girl screaming bloody murder. The sound was coming from the basement. "Help me!" she yelled over and over again. "Somebody please help me!"

I knew it was Gina. With all of my heart I wanted to go down there and save her. I wanted her to know that someone did hear her, that if she could just hold on for another minute, help was on the way. But with two huge chains wrapped around my body, all I could do was listen to her screams— and wonder why no one ever heard any of us.

# 16

# The Third Girl

FOR THE REST of April I didn't hear another sound from the basement. The silence was creepy; it worried me to death. And what made it even worse was seeing Mayra on the news begging everyone to help her find her little sister. I asked myself over and over: *Is Gina down there in the helmet? Is she struggling to breathe? Has Amanda seen her? Will I ever see her? Is she still alive?* I had no clue.

Finally, one night I looked directly at the dude and said, "I know you took that girl." He stared at me but didn't answer. I was surprised he didn't knock me in the head.

A week or so later the dude came into my room and handed me a red spiral notebook, a pencil, and a small sharpener. "Here, maybe you can draw or something," he said.

The pencil was dull, but it had an eraser on the bottom. Some of the pages of the notebook were torn out. I didn't thank him. I just took the pencil, notebook, and sharpener out of his hand. On the inside I was yelling, "Oh my god! I can't believe it! Now I can draw! Yes!" This was the first day in that house, other than the days I got Lobo and the TV, when something good happened.

After he left, it felt weird to even hold the pencil in my fingers. I hadn't held a pencil or a pen for over a year. My fingers shook. I was scared because I kept thinking I heard the dude on the stairs, and I didn't want him to take the notebook away from me. I never knew when he would change his mind about something. I really missed drawing wolves, so right away I drew one. I made it so big that it filled the whole page and went over the edges a little. It wasn't my best one, but I was still happy.

From then on, the first thing I did when I woke up was pick up that pencil, sharpen it, and start writing or drawing. I couldn't get enough; I wrote every day. Poems. Songs. What made me sad. Letters to Joey. And dreams of how I wished everything could be different. I was careful not to say anything too specific about the dude, because I figured he might read it.

This is one of the first things I wrote:

*Every time I see a butterfly, it reminds me of how precious life can truly be. To be able to turn from a caterpillar into a beautiful butterfly and fly away so freely and gracefully wherever she may please, without no one in the world to tell her what to do. I wait for that special moment in time when I get to live life freely, without no worries, pain, or tears. I just want to be happy. I want to hear the laughter in the air without all of the pain. One special day I'll get to live my life just like that beautiful butterfly. I will no longer feel blue inside.*

The only time I got interrupted was when the dude came in. I didn't want him to read what I wrote or take away the notebook, so I hid it under my pillow.

A few days after he gave me the notebook the movie *101 Dalmatians* was on TV. I cried the whole time because it reminded me of Joey. I missed him more than you can imagine. Only a mother can understand what it's like to have her child torn away from her. It's like having your soul ripped right out of your body. You can barely speak because it hurts so bad. To try to get rid of some of the pain, I wrote to my huggy bear:

> *I am sitting here watching* 101 Dalmatians *and remembering that it's your favorite movie. You loved to watch it over and over again ... I miss you, baby. I wish I could hug you right now. I wish I could watch the movie with you and see you laugh. One day I will see you again. I love you with all of my heart.*

Right after I wrote that, I closed the notebook and held it up to my chest. Before long I was asleep. That night I dreamed the same dream I'd had before—my sweet Joey being dragged away from me and disappearing forever.

ONE MORNING AROUND the middle of May the dude came in with his drill and told me to get up. "You're going to help me prepare the room," he said, and he started drilling another hole in my wall. I was pretty sure I knew the reason why.

I had been wondering what was going on with Gina, although I hadn't heard anything else from the basement. I hoped that she was surviving all right, but I knew what an animal he was. It tore me up inside to think of a fourteen-year-old girl going through what he'd put me through. At times I had wondered if she had survived.

When he forced me to put a second set of chains through the wall, I begged him, "Please, don't make me help you commit a crime!"

"You won't get blamed for it," he said. "It's all on me." By saying that, he admitted what I had already figured out: he had snatched Gina. He took out my bucket and returned with one of those little white portable toilets and put it next to the mattress. I assumed he was doing this because it was slightly bigger, and two people would now be using it.

I thought I would see Gina that day, but another couple of weeks went by. Then, out of nowhere, the dude brought her into my room. At first I wasn't quite sure if it was really Gina DeJesus. She had on baggy sweatpants and a T-shirt. They looked like the same kind of stinky, dingy men's clothes that he sometimes gave me. She was barefoot. Her long, thick, black hair went all the way down past her shoulders. She seemed so young; she had a baby face. She looked scared, almost like she was holding her breath. I was glad that at least I had on a tank top and underwear.

"This is my daughter," he said, pushing her toward the mattress.

*God, what a liar!* I thought. *I guess the idiot doesn't remember he'd asked me to prepare those chains.*

"Hi," she finally said.

"Hi," I said back. Gina's eyes looked incredibly sad. Although I went to high school with Gina's older sister, Mayra, I didn't really know her that well. We weren't really friends; we just saw each other around our neighborhood and at school. Sometimes she waved and said "Hi." Once, Mayra had showed me a picture of her baby sister. Another time I saw her walking with Gina not too far from my house.

Now that I was seeing Gina again after all that time, I had to take a close look at her face to see if it was really her. From the pictures in the news reports, I was pretty sure it was. I was getting ready to ask her how she was doing. Before we could say another word, the dude turned her around and took her out of the room with him.

*Why did he do that?* I wondered. I had no idea whether I'd ever see her again. If she had to be stuck in this house, I hoped at least we could be together. My heart went out to her; I knew how scared and lonely she must be feeling. I wanted to help her in any way I could. And after spending all those months by myself, I wanted to talk to someone—anyone other than the monster. Of course, I wished Gina wasn't there, and the same thing with Amanda. Just thinking about someone else living in that hellhole made my stomach hurt. I laid back down, worrying about poor Gina and also wondering how Amanda was doing. *Maybe with three of us in the house, we'll have a better chance of escaping,* I thought. *Maybe we can all team up and kick his butt, then make a break for it.*

A few days later the dude unchained me and took me downstairs to the bathroom. When he opened the door, Gina was standing there. "She's gonna do your hair," he told me.

I thought, *Why on earth is he having Gina do my hair?* I didn't know what he was talking about, but then again, most of what he did made no sense. But I had learned how to play along with his weird ideas to avoid getting beaten. *Maybe I'll get some time alone with Gina to ask her how she's doing,* I thought. I went over to the toilet, closed the lid, and sat down. As before, the whole thing shook a little when I sat on it.

"Go ahead," he said to Gina. "Do her hair."

Gina took a couple of pieces of my hair, which was short from when I'd cut it, and started making a twist at the front of my head. A couple of seconds later the dude walked away. I motioned to Gina to put her head down toward me, and I put my mouth right up to her ear.

"I know who you are," I said as softly as I could. "You're Gina DeJesus." I didn't want him to hear me, come back in, and knock us both out.

She straightened up and looked me right in the eyes. "You *know* me?" she whispered. She seemed surprised. I nodded. She looked over her shoulder at the door, then she started twisting my hair again.

"Don't tell him that I know who you are," I warned her. "It might piss him off. When I get a chance to tell you more about him and the situation, I will." Right then the dude came back inside. We both acted like we hadn't been talking. *That was close,* I thought.

That first conversation with Gina had lasted less than thirty seconds. For the next five minutes the dude stood there and watched her twist my hair. When it was done, I got up and looked in the bathroom mirror. The twists were beautiful.

"Thank you," I said to her.

The dude seemed annoyed at that. He yanked me over to the door, took us both back upstairs, and chained me to the bed. Then he went back downstairs with Gina. I don't know where he took her. Maybe down to the basement. Maybe to his cubbyhole. I hoped it was out the front door and back to her life, but I knew better than that.

A few days later the dude brought Gina back into my room. She looked even more pale and wiped out than she did the first time I'd seen her.

"Get on the bed," he told her. Without a word she sat down beside me. He chained me by the neck, and then he wrapped the same chains around her ankle. Gina asked him to switch the chains. "It's not going to work if my leg is chained to her neck—how are we supposed to use the toilet?" she said. I was glad she had spoken up.

"Her ankle's too small," he said. "If I put it around her foot, she'll get out."

But Gina kept asking him, and I could hardly believe it when he actually listened to her. He took the chain off my neck and then chained us together by our feet. Of course, he made my foot chain very tight. After that, he tossed another pair of sweats and a couple of ugly T-shirts at me.

"These are for you," he said. I guess he wanted me to have more clothes because Gina was with me, but of course I wouldn't be able to put on the sweatpants until he unchained us. After that, he left.

We heard his boots go down the stairs. *Pound. Pound. Pound.* We were together in chains. In tears. For a long time we sat and listened to the house get quiet. Then we began telling each other our whole stories.

Kindergarten

First grade

Fifth grade

Junior high

Freshman year in high school

TOP: One of the houses I lived in with my family. MIDDLE: The bridge I lived under when I was homeless. (*Both photos courtesy of Robert Friedrick*) BOTTOM: Castro's house. (*© AP Images/Tony Dejak*)

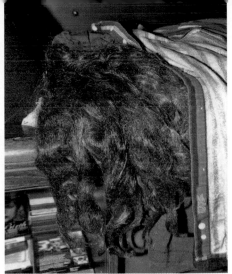

TOP LEFT: The heavy motorcycle helmet that the dude put on my head. (© *AP Images/Tony Dejak*)

TOP RIGHT: The wig that he put on me when he took me outside on the porch. (© *AP Images/Tony Dejak*)

LEFT: The nasty basement where I was chained to a pole. (© *AP Images/Tony Dejak*)

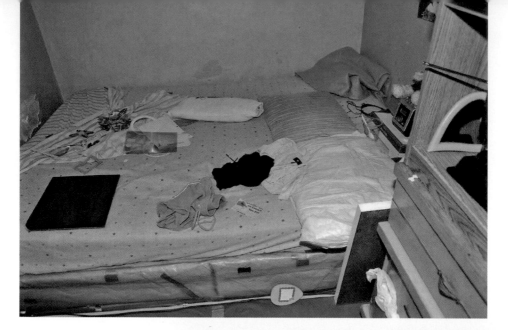

ABOVE: The mattress in the pink bedroom, where I was tortured for years. (© *AP Images/Tony Dejak*)

RIGHT: Chain coming out of the pink bedroom wall. (© *AP Images/Tony Dejak*)

BELOW: Chains and padlocks. (© *AP Images/ Tony Dejak*)

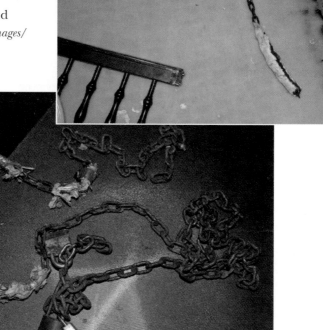

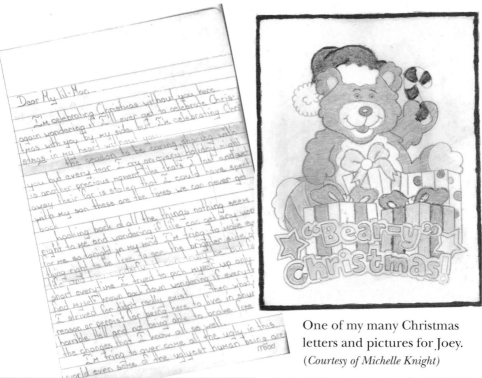

One of my many Christmas letters and pictures for Joey. (*Courtesy of Michelle Knight*)

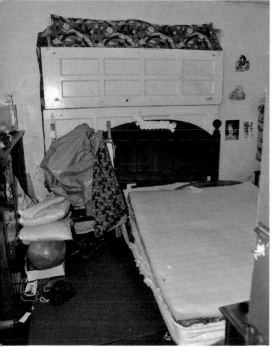

The white bedroom that connected to the pink bedroom. (© *AP Images/ Tony Dejak*)

The dude's filthy bathroom. (© *AP Images/Tony Dejak*)

The door with heavy curtain that led downstairs to the first floor. (© AP Images/Tony Dejak)

Alarms that the dude rigged up on the front door. (© AP Images/Tony Dejak)

Testifying against the dude in court. (© AP Images/Tony Dejak)

One of my good friends,
Pastor Angel Arroyo, Jr.
(*Courtesy of Luis Gonzalez, Sr.*)

With one of my heroes, Dr. Phil.
(*Courtesy of* Dr. Phil Show/*Jared Manders*)

With my lawyer Peggy and my friend Tricia. (*Courtesy of Deborah Feingold*)

At my first Broadway show, *Kinky Boots,* with actor Billy Porter, who played Lola. (*Courtesy of Lacy Lalene Lynch*)

Here I am at culinary school. (*Courtesy of Linda Fazio*)

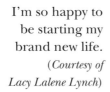

I'm so happy to be starting my brand new life. (*Courtesy of Lacy Lalene Lynch*)

# 17

## My New Little Sister

*I can imagine the pain of having a missing child. To not
know where they are at or what horrible things they are going
through. Knowing you can't be there to hold and protect
her from the damage that's being caused … I can imagine
having the strength I do now to hold my head up high
through this pain after all these years without falling on my
knees. In my eyes I am amazing for having the courage to
believe there's something bigger than a life full of misery.*

How do you start telling another victim what it was like to
be kidnapped off the street and turned into a prisoner in
a strange man's house? It's overwhelming. And just going
through the whole story makes you want to scream.

I had so many things I wanted to ask Gina, such as whether
she knew there was a third girl in the house, how she was
feeling, and if he had been feeding her enough. There were
so many things I wanted to tell her and also to warn her
about—like what made him mad and that he would pretend

to go out but then sneak back in to see if you were trying to get loose.

For the first couple of minutes we didn't say too much. I think we were both so stunned by the situation and also by finally having someone to talk to. It took a minute to get used to that idea. Then I picked up where we left off in the bathroom. I told her that I knew her older sister, Mayra, from school.

Gina's pretty brown eyes got wide. "You did?" she said.

I nodded. After that, the words just started flowing between us. The first thing I asked her was, "How did he get you into the house?"

Gina cleared her throat and talked very softly. I scooted next to her so she wouldn't have to speak any louder. Neither one of us wanted the dude to come running back upstairs. "I was walking down the street with Rosie," Gina told me. I knew that Rosie was the dude's daughter. Gina and Rosie were the best of friends; their families knew each other. Gina had spent the night at Rosie's mother's house, and Rosie had stayed at Gina's. Around three o'clock the two of them were walking home from middle school.

"We stopped at a pay phone to call Rosie's mom and asked if I could go over to her house that night," Gina told me. The pay phone they used was close to 105th Street and Lorain Avenue, in the same area where both Amanda and I were taken. When Rosie's mom said no, Gina and Rosie said good-bye to each other and walked in different directions.

While Gina was walking home, the dude pulled up next to her and told her he was looking for Rosie. Gina had seen the dude before and knew he was Rosie's father. Gina wanted to help him find his daughter, so she got in the car and pointed him in the direction Rosie had been walking. But the dude started driving in a different direction, so she told him again which way Rosie had gone.

"I just gotta go back to my house and pick up something," he told her. "Maybe you and my other daughter Emily can go to the mall together later." Gina knew Emily, but she still thought saying that was kind of strange because he had just told her he was looking for Rosie. But just like me, she shrugged it off and trusted the dude because he was the father of her good friend.

When they pulled up at his house, he even handed her some cash. "Here's some money for you and Emily to spend at the mall," he told her. He then got her to come into the house and forced her down into the basement. Sitting on the mattress with our ankles chained together, I told Gina how the dude had tricked me into coming to the house and how it was like the way he'd lured her in. I told her how long I'd been chained up there. I told her I'd been there for two years and that my son wasn't with me but, instead, was in foster care. But I didn't tell her a lot about the horrible stuff he did to me after I got there because I thought it would scare her. She looked so innocent; I just wanted to protect her. Every time I looked at her sweet young face, her beautiful brown eyes, and long dark hair, it made me so mad and so angry. How could anyone take this girl away from her family? And what kind of father do you have to be to kidnap your daughter's best friend? You have to be a demon—and that's exactly what he was.

That night I told Gina that Amanda was also in the house. Gina replied that she had already seen her, but they hadn't really talked yet.

"I haven't gotten the chance to talk to her either," I said. "She must be so scared." We couldn't believe this guy had gotten away with *three* kidnappings. All in the same neighborhood. And all three of us knew his children. Why wasn't anyone putting all of this together?

"Do you think we will ever get out?" Gina asked me. I hesitated. Although I hoped this was true, by that point I wasn't sure. I'd been either chained tightly to the wall or watched closely every minute of the almost two years I'd been in the house.

"Yes," I finally said. I wanted Gina to have hope.

"Well, we just have to try," she said. I knew she was right.

We started talking about our lives, and after we finished telling each other our stories, we just sat there and cried, holding onto each other.

"I never should have got in his truck," I told her. "I never would have taken a ride from a total stranger. But I let down my guard because he was Emily's dad." Seeing a big fat tear rolling down Gina's face, I wiped it away with my hand. "It'll be okay, sweetie," I told her. "We'll get through this. Now that there are three of us in here, we'll find a way out. We have to."

Having Gina in the house meant that her life had been taken away too. But if she had to be locked in this monster's hellhole, I was glad she wasn't alone, shivering in the basement. If we were stuck here, at least we could be with each other. Maybe we really could escape if we put our heads together. All along it had been the thought of Joey that had kept me fighting to stay alive. And now I had a little sister to fight for too.

*I'm just a girl hidden away from the rest of the world, not where I expected to be. Stuck in this nightmare, screaming, only to find out no one can hear me. All I ask in return is to be with my son, safe ... but the reality is slipping from my grasp. I'm thinking that was too much to ask. Life goes past me so quickly, my health is fading fast, then I run away into my deepest sleep and dream of paradise.*

EVEN BEFORE THE dude brought Gina to my room, getting over to the pot to pee was hard. I had to stretch to reach it. But after Gina and I were chained up together, it became even harder. If one of us got up, the other one had to move too. From the minute she came to the room we learned to depend on each other for everything, even going to the bathroom.

"He hardly ever empties it," I warned her. But I'm sure the gross smell told her that already. Our pot often got so full that it overflowed. One time I peed into a beer bottle. Gina was like, "How in the world did you do *that*?" It was very weird doing such private stuff in front of each other. But we got used to it. We didn't have a choice.

In the mornings the dude came upstairs and gave us something to eat, usually still an egg sandwich from a fast food restaurant. For the first couple of weeks he didn't have sex with me in the room, and he didn't hit me. I think it was because he didn't want to scare Gina. Matter of fact, I don't even think he meant to kidnap Gina in the first place.

One time, when he took me downstairs to his cubbyhole, he was drunk as hell on rum. He tried to get me to drink some shots too, but I said no. He was almost passed out on his bed when he started telling me a lot more about how he picked Gina.

"Every day when she left school, I followed her," he said. "I followed all three of you." When he said that, it really gave me the creeps. He also told me there was another girl in Gina's school who looked exactly like her, and he got the two of them confused. He said he didn't know that he'd kidnapped his daughter's friend until he saw Gina's name on the news. Then again, he didn't feel too bad about it. He also told me that later on he even helped Gina's parents search for her. The whole time he knew exactly where she was, but while they prayed and cried and looked all over the city, he played along like he was a friend. He really got off on it—that's how evil and twisted this man was.

Another time when we were in his room a report came on about Gina's disappearance. "They're looking for her, but they'll never find her," he laughed. And of course he had to remind me again, "No one was ever looking for you. That's why I hate you the most. You ain't nothin' to nobody. Nobody loves you, and nobody misses you." I tried not to show it, but that really hurt. It made me wonder yet again if anyone in my family had ever tried to find me or even missed me. It gave me such a hopeless, hollow feeling inside.

I didn't tell Gina any of this; I thought it might make her even more sad. When you're the oldest one, you have to watch out for the younger ones. That's just what big sisters do.

We both knew he was out of his mind, but at first Gina didn't believe he was as mean as I knew he was. That was because he really didn't abuse her that much in the beginning. For a while he wouldn't hit me in the head if she was in the room.

"He's being fake right now," I told her. "Just watch yourself around him. He's a psycho."

Sure enough, things got bad after about a month. One night he raped me while I was chained to Gina. She sat in the corner of the mattress and tried to look the other way. After it was over, we just sat there and cried.

Throughout the next many months and years the same thing would happen over and over again. The dude would take either me or Gina off to the side of the bed; the other one would sit there feeling helpless to stop it. If I tried to say anything, he'd just reach over and punch me in the face, and then take it out on Gina more. Sometimes we would reach out and touch each other's hand and say, "It's going to be okay." He didn't try to stop us from doing that. Other times, if the dude started in with Gina, I would beg for him to stop.

"Please, take me instead," I said. "I'm the one you hate."

It's one thing to have someone break your own heart; it can be even more painful to watch another person's heart get crushed. During all the time I shared a room with Gina my heart was smashed in half too many different times to count. I don't think I can ever really get over what both of us went through.

WE STILL DIDN'T see Amanda very much in the months after Gina arrived in April. The dude started letting us shower downstairs every once in a while, so we just said hi when we passed each other. Gina and Amanda kind of stared at each other, because they had never had a conversation. Sometimes when we were chained together upstairs on the mattress, we could hear him taking Amanda down the stairs to his cubbyhole. It was weird knowing that another girl was probably going through all the horrible stuff I was going through, but we never had the chance to sit down and talk. I didn't know it then, but a number of months would go by before Amanda and I would finally get that chance.

Over the first few months I told Gina everything I had learned about the dude. "He's got two sides to his personality," I warned her. "You never know which one you're gonna get." I also explained what all the sounds meant—like the voices that meant his band had come over for the weekend. The scared look on Gina's face said it all: *Am I going to be here so long that I need to know all this?* When I saw how frightened she seemed, I held back some things. I knew she was scared enough already, but I also wanted her to have some information that might protect her.

To make the days go by faster, Gina and I watched a lot of TV together. "The volume doesn't work very well," I told her the first time she turned it on. "And whatever you do, don't let the dude catch you watching black people on TV. He hates black folks." We loved to watch shows about celebrities because it took our minds off of our situation to keep up with the latest gossip. It kind of made me feel human again. And we liked *The Parkers*, *The Fresh Prince of Bel-Air*, and *Friends*. At least we were looking at the same things the rest of the world was looking at, even if we were locked up in a prison.

Sometimes, after a couple of hours of watching sitcoms or stupid reruns, I would get out my notebook. The dude had given Gina a notebook and a pencil too. We would draw and write until we ran out of pages. Believe it or not, if we asked him for more notebooks, sometimes he would give them to us. We both thought it was weird, but we were just glad to have them. At times we'd read what we'd written out loud to each other. Gina liked to draw flowers and faces, and sometimes I'd help her out with the eyes in one of her pictures. She liked my drawings and said that I was good at art.

Once, I was writing about him in my notebook as he came through the door. He saw me push it under my pillow. "What are you writing?" he said.

Gina and I looked at each other out of the corner of our eyes. He was acting angry about something.

"You want to read it?" I said, trying to play it off.

He grabbed the notebook. On that page I had written about how he had treated me the Christmas before and how much I hated him for everything he did to me.

"Sometimes I cry so hard, and I just want to die," I wrote. "All I want to do is go home. All I want to do is see Joey. I still can't believe this monster had stolen away my life."

After he read that, he stopped and looked at me for a long time. "So you're trying to tell me I'm a bastard?" he said.

I stared down at the mattress. "I'm not saying anything to you," I told him. "You're the one who said you wanted to read the notebook—so read it."

After I said that, I backed up a little on the bed because I knew what might come next: a smack in the jaw. But he didn't hit me. Matter of fact, he seemed a little sad and weepy. In some strange way I really think the dude believed that his pretend world was real. He knew it was wrong to kidnap us, but he tried to convince himself that what he was doing to us was okay, because in his twisted mind he had turned us into his "family." Every now and then, though, he got a huge reminder of how much I hated him. And the day he read my notebook he got one of those reminders. He never asked to see my journal again, and I was just grateful he didn't take it away from me.

*I am falling in the dark, falling so hard with these open scars and a bruised heart. I am paralyzed. How did I read the signs so wrong, and why couldn't I figure it out before it was too late? Now it's clear to me that everything you see ain't always what it appears to be. I am paralyzed ... God knows how I've tried to see the brighter side of this Hell, but now I am awake. The darkness doesn't blind me ... now the pain will fade away and never return.*

# 18

## Voices

*Being told to do things even though it hurts you. Feeling in life no one cares about you. Always feeling very tired and staying up for too many days feeling sick to my stomach. Having aches and pain all over, feels like my head is about to explode, screaming someone help me before it is too late. Tears always falling from my cheek, hoping this will end soon and someone will rescue me, but it feels like this will never end. I don't understand why a person can be so heartless.*

One wicked hot day that summer Gina and I were both writing in our notebooks. We were dripping with sweat, wearing tank tops and shorts. Suddenly I heard voices downstairs. They sounded different from the guys in the band. For one thing, I could hear a little child say something.

"What was *that*?" I whispered to Gina. We stopped writing and put down our notebooks.

The dude came up the stairs and opened our door. "I'm going to let you meet my grandson," he said.

Really? We're meeting someone in your family? You really must have flipped out! Gina and I glanced at each other quickly, and then back at him.

"My daughter Angie's son is here," he said. "Hide your chains. He's really young, so it's okay for him to meet you."

Without another word, we stuffed our chains behind the back of the mattress.

"If you try to yell," he said with a menacing look, "I'll run up here and shoot you both. And Amanda too. Don't think I won't do it."

He walked out and went back down the stairs. This was unbelievably weird—the lunatic was going to let his grandson see us? What would happen? Would Angie come upstairs too, if she was here? Gina and I looked at each other, not believing this was happening.

"Do you think we'll be able to get out?" she whispered.

"I hope so!" I said in a low voice. "But don't let the dude see what we're thinking. And we'd better not try to call out to anyone. He was serious about shooting us. He's enough of a wacko to do it, even if his family is downstairs. Hopefully the kid will tell his mother we're up here."

A minute later we heard the dude's boots on the stairs, and then I heard him introducing his grandson to Amanda. Right after that, the dude came through our door holding the hand of the boy. The little guy had dark hair and a cute, round face with chipmunk cheeks. He looked like he was around three or four years old. Seeing him immediately made me miss my Joey even more.

"This is my grandson," he told us. He smiled and seemed very proud to be showing off the boy to us.

Gina and I waved to him, and I said, "Aw, you're so cute."
I thought about trying to say something that would let the
boy know we were being held against our will, but I couldn't
come up with anything fast enough. That kid took one long
look at the two of us and got this very weird look on his face,
like he just knew there was something wrong with us being
up there.

All of sudden he started crying hysterically. "Mommy!" he
yelled. "Mommy, come get me!"

The dude tried to shut him up. "Shhhh, you can't do
that!" he said. He put his huge, hairy hand over the boy's
mouth. It looked like the kid was trying to run back downstairs. I also heard other people, so I figured that some of the
dude's family was there. But before Angie or whoever was in
the house could come up to see why the kid was crying, the
dude rushed him back downstairs.

*What was that all about?* I thought. *Why the heck would he let
anyone in his family know that we're up here?* I figured maybe taking a risk like that gave the dude a sick thrill, like the way he
flaunted it that he was smarter than the cops and hadn't gotten caught. But I didn't really care why. All I cared about was
that someone had finally seen us, even if it was just a little kid.

After a while we heard the people leaving the house. Gina
and I were excited. We'd be rescued now, for sure! The kid
would tell his mother or others in the family, and they'd
come to investigate. We could hardly sleep that night for
thinking of what we'd do when we got out. She couldn't wait
to see her family again. I couldn't wait to see Joey.

"Social services is going to be my first stop, once I can
make a phone call," I told her.

But no one showed up the next day, or the next. A couple of days later I was chained up in his cubbyhole while he was in the kitchen, having a conversation on his phone. It seemed like he was talking to someone in his family. "No, the house ain't ready," he told whoever it was. "I need to clean up." Although the person seemed to be insisting on coming by, the dude continued to say no. And then finally he said, "Maybe you can come by in a few days. Just let me get some stuff cleaned up."

As soon as I heard him say that, something clicked. Kids are smart—and that little boy was definitely smart enough to know that something was wrong. I wondered whether he had told his mom or other family members about meeting us. If so, maybe that made Angie, or whoever was on the phone, suspicious. Maybe she wondered whether something was off with her dad and wanted to come by to check it out for herself. *Maybe.*

That night I could hardly sleep for hoping we were about to be rescued. I fantasized about seeing Joey again. I imagined what it would be like not to have these chains biting into my flesh twenty-four hours a day. I thought about taking a long, hot shower, eating food that wasn't spoiled. Surely we were about to be set free! But again in the following days nothing at all happened.

About two weeks later the dude came upstairs and unlocked us. "You're going down into the basement," he told us.

I didn't say anything to Gina, but I'm sure the look on my face told her everything: the thought of going back down into that dungeon scared the crap out of me. And there was another surprise that day: he made *all three* of us walk down those old dusty stairs together. He chained all of us to the pole by our necks and stomachs. He then crammed a filthy sock into each of our mouths and wound duct tape around our heads.

"If any of you makes a sound," he said in a low voice, "I'll shoot all three of you." I guess by "sound" he meant moaning, because we were gagged. He then turned off the light. After he left I could hear him padlocking the door.

This was the very first time the three of us were in the same room alone together, but we were chained and gagged. It was frustrating not to be able to communicate. I was back where I'd started on that filthy basement floor, chained with my back to the pole. I tried to work the sock out of my mouth, but the duct tape was too tight.

Not long afterward I heard voices from upstairs. I think it was the dude's family—it sounded like the same group of voices I heard on that day the grandson met us. I don't know for sure if Angie was there, but I definitely heard her little boy. My heart nearly stopped beating and I held my breath through the dirty sock.

"What's down here?" I heard a woman's voice say. "Can you unlock this?"

There was a long pause. "I can't," the dude said. "It's messy down there. There's water all over the floor. I'm doing some work down there."

I let out all the air through my nose. There was no way in hell the dude would ever open that door.

But whoever was there, why didn't they call the cops right at that moment? Didn't the person's gut tell her something seemed fishy? When I think about it now I am so furious. We came *this close* to being found, but because someone didn't call the police, we were still held prisoner in that bastard's house.

Eventually the voices upstairs stopped, and I figured they'd left. I also thought they would go home and call the police, because they decided not to do it right then. Later the dude came down and removed our gags, gave us a little food, and then went back upstairs.

"Amanda, how are you doing in here—are you okay?" I asked after he left.

"I'm okay, I guess," she said softly.

Gina and I took turns telling her the stories we had told each other—how we got kidnapped and what kinds of terrible things the dude had been doing to us.

"What about you?" I asked her.

She told us a little bit about how she was kidnapped. The dude offered her a ride home from her job at Burger King and then forced her into the house. When we confided in her about what the dude had done to us, she just said something like, "Yeah, same here."

I figured Amanda was too scared or exhausted to talk. I felt sorry for her. "Well, all I know is that I don't want to die here," I finally said. I began to cry. I couldn't stop myself—the water just came pouring out. "We've all got to be friends to each other. We have to find a way to get out of this rat hole. Now that we have each other, we have to stick together until we're rescued. Maybe whoever was upstairs is calling the cops right now to come check it out."

But yet again, no one came. And for about two weeks the three of us were chained together in that basement. The dude eventually loosened our chains a little and moved the piss bucket closer. If he wanted to have sex with one of us, he came down and took one of us back upstairs. In between all that, we talked a lot. We tried to think about ideas of how we could get out of there. We didn't really have any great ideas; it's hard to get free when you're always chained up. Still, we tried to be imaginative about it. At least it helped to pass the time.

After more than two weeks of being stuck in that basement the dude finally took us back upstairs. Gina and I were still chained together in one room, and Amanda was in her own room. It seemed like we were back where we started before his grandson saw us. I just couldn't believe someone hadn't come to set us free.

*I want to celebrate my homecoming, not my funeral. I still have so much I want to say and do. Life is too short not to live it right … from this day forward I will embrace everything good and desecrate all that is evil. I've seen enough evil to last a lifetime now. I want the good in life without worrying. To be with people who are caring, smiles that last for miles, and love that's forever lasting, a home that I call my own, not a prison. I may be defeated and beaten down, only to get back up again, to stand tall with head held high and my pride not shaken. Only to survive this horrible nightmare with my heart still attached and my soul not stolen and walk away without a scar on me.*

# 19

## The Van

*I love life … My son is the most precious to me. I will give up anything to be with my son at home where I belong … Life changes from good to bad … in a blink of an eye your whole life can change, so you should live life like it's your last days on earth because you never know when tragedy might strike. … Some people don't have a family to turn to in time of need … I can't wait for this nightmare to end so I can wake up and be me again.*

A couple of weeks later, one morning before the sun was even up, the dude dragged us down the stairs.

"I'm moving you into my van 'cause my family is coming over here soon," he told us. His family had been to the house before, of course, so I figured he wanted to get us out of the room so he could show them around again. He probably wanted to prove to Angie, or whoever had been in the kitchen, that nothing strange was going on.

He had a large burgundy van parked in his backyard, one I'd seen there a few times before. He pushed us out the back door and into the yard. I looked around, hoping someone would see us, but no one seemed to be around this early in the morning. As soon as we climbed in, it was pretty clear he had planned this. The inside was big enough for about twelve people to sit. He had chains looped around the bottom of the seats in the middle. The two backseats had been removed, and there was a place to lie down. It smelled really bad in there. Under the rearview mirror hung a little sign that said "Puerto Rico," the country where his family was from.

He locked up Gina and me together on the seats, and he chained Amanda by herself in back. Our chains were just long enough so we could use a portable pot he put in there, but they weren't long enough to allow us to stand up and look out of the tinted windows. Before he shut the door he said, "If I hear a sound, I will come out here and kill all three of you."

It was hotter than hell in that van. I passed out a couple of times from the summer heat. Most of the time I just slept. The dude didn't let us have our notebooks or pencils, so I couldn't even draw or write to Joey. My T-shirt was so wet with sweat that you could see through it. But then again, I was grateful to have a shirt on to soak up the sweat. I thought about all those days when I had laid dirty and naked on the basement floor. As bad as this was, that was even worse.

We stayed in the van for five days. On the first day the dude kept checking to make sure we weren't trying to get loose or calling for help. And he gave us a little food and water. I was surprised and relieved when he didn't make any of us have sex with him or take anyone back into the house. In the house he often forced himself on me twice a day, but that week he left me alone.

Early in the morning of the fourth day I heard him get into the van. I pretended like I was asleep, hoping he would just leave. He stayed in the back and whispered to Amanda for a while. I could see a bit of what happened next, but then I closed my eyes real tight. The only thing more horrible than being raped is watching it happen to someone else.

I didn't know if the dude's family ever came to the house. But he checked on us often, and I knew he had the gun. I thought about screaming, trying to attract attention from a neighbor or someone passing by, but he was in and out of the van unpredictably. He had me convinced that if he heard us yelling, he'd get to us and shoot us before anyone could find us. And by that time, after being chained up, raped, and beaten constantly for over two years, I thought he was capable of anything. I definitely believed he would shoot all of us in cold blood, even if help was on the way.

Sometimes I almost thought that dying that way would be a relief, after what I'd gone through. At least it would happen instantly. And sometimes I felt like God had abandoned me. But then I would think of Joey, and I'd know there was a reason I was still here. And I didn't want to do something that would get Gina and Amanda killed. So I suffered through those sweltering days in the van without screaming for help. I knew he could be out the door and in the van with his gun in seconds.

When the dude finally unchained us, he took us back inside the house and upstairs to our rooms. It was still a prison up there, but at least it was a prison that included spiral notebooks, pencils, and *Everybody Loves Raymond*. And although it was hot upstairs in the rooms with the boarded-up windows, it wasn't quite as sweltering as it had been in the van.

During TV commercials Gina and I fantasized about all the different ways we could try to escape. I remembered that he had a guitar in his cubbyhole. "Maybe we could tie him up with one of his guitar strings while he's asleep," I said, ignoring the fact that this would be pretty much impossible to do because we were chained to the bed. Gina just looked at me. Okay, so that probably wasn't the greatest idea. "Or how about trying to stab him?" I continued. "Maybe if he fell asleep, I could sneak into the kitchen and get a knife."

Gina nodded. "Then after you did," she said, "we could get Amanda loose and finally get out of here." A minute later, when our show was back on, we went back to watching TV. Deep down inside I think we both knew our plans were not going to work. How could we even dream of getting away when he kept us chained up 99 percent of the time? But I had to keep thinking of new plans for escaping. It was one of the only ways I could keep myself from going crazy. You have to have something to hope for.

*Mirror hanging on the wall, you don't see my true reflection at all. If you did, you would know that I was the loneliest girl of them all, walking on fire while I stand alone in the mirror of a life that isn't mine ... having the thought of never going home so deep within my heart, while waiting for my world to stop falling apart.*

*Even though my heart isn't made out of glass, my heart still fills with pain and shatters into pieces like my heart was made to break ... I'm the one who's lost. I know you will be so quick to break me fast. I feel my heart beating when I think about the past. I wish I could throw these broken*

*thoughts in the trash, to never be thought of again … If I
can make everything feel right again, can you imagine how
my story would end? Then I can mend my broken wings so I
can finally feel the sweetness of life instead of the bitter taste
of sin that lurks around, waiting for their next victim to
strike down.*

TOWARD THE END of 2004 we started getting a little more
freedom to move around the house as long as the dude was
right there with us. He would take us downstairs to make
dinner, always carrying his gun. A couple of times I thought
about trying to make a run for the back door, but I was too
afraid he would shoot me from behind and then kill everyone else. I also remembered the times when he would leave
a door unlocked to see if he could catch me trying to get
out. He seemed to always be testing us, ready to pounce if he
caught us even looking at the door.

The kitchen was as much of a hot mess as the rest of the
house. The stove had stains all over it from spilled food that
he never cleaned up. There was a stack of old pots and pans
on a chair next to the stove. Gina did most of the cooking.
Even if I wanted to cook, I couldn't reach the cabinets, so
he made me stand over in a corner. A lot of times, while
Gina and I were down in the kitchen, the dude would sit at
the dining room table with Amanda and talk to her in a low
voice. I could just imagine what kind of idiotic things he was
saying.

The meal was almost always the same: rice and beans. The
beans could be any color: black, red, pink. They all came

from Goya cans. The white rice was the cheap junk, the kind you pour out of a box. Every now and then I saw little bugs in the rice. *Gross.* After Gina and I ate and cleaned up the mess, Amanda had to cook her own beans and rice while we sat in the kitchen. I don't know why he had us eat separately sometimes; only God knows.

After everybody was done eating, the dude would keep us downstairs for a while. He often gave us a bunch of Coronas or some shots of rum. When I first came into the house he had tried to give me liquor. I didn't take it back then, wanting to keep my mind clear. But by the time the other girls got there, I *needed* a drink. I didn't even really like the taste, but at least it was *something* to blot out the pain. It was one of the only ways I could make myself forget about the horror I was living through. Why try to stay sober when you feel like you're dying?

I knew he wasn't giving us alcohol to be *nice* to us—no way. He just wanted to get us so drunk that we'd loosen up and do all kinds of nasty things with him. Gina and I often talked about how we could wait until he was too drunk to stand up and then escape while he was passed out on the floor. Unfortunately, that never happened. Even after he had a lot to drink, he would sit there calmly, always watching us.

One night, when we'd all had too much beer, he handed me his gun. "Shoot me," he said with a straight face.

I didn't move. I wondered if there were really any bullets in the gun.

"That's a retarded game," I finally said. I was pretty sure this was some kind of sick trick. Then he snatched the gun out of my hand and put it up to my head.

"Don't do it!" I yelled. "Please don't shoot me!" My whole body started to shake. He went to pull the trigger, but before he could fire, I knocked the gun out of his hand. It flew across the kitchen. When it landed on the floor, a couple of bullets came spilling out. *Oh my God, it really was loaded!*

I was so frightened that I fainted right there onto the kitchen floor. When I woke up from my blackout, I found myself back upstairs, chained to Gina. I wasn't surprised that the dude put the gun to my head. After Amanda and Gina got there, I had turned into the most hated girl in the house. He started treating me worse and worse, if that was possible. He would constantly push me down the stairs, beat me and punch me, or cuss me out. And every time he was done making me bleed, he would remind me, "You're such an ugly bitch. You're the one I can't stand to look at." And then he'd add, "At least I didn't kill you."

He also abused Gina and Amanda. I don't know exactly what he was doing to Amanda, since she wasn't in our room, but I'm pretty sure he was forcing himself on her too. Sometimes I could hear it happening. But even though we all got treated horribly, I got hit upside the head the most. And I was raped two and sometimes even three or four times a day.

I felt so low and dirty. Other than Joey and maybe my brothers, I couldn't think of anyone who probably missed me all that much. *Even if I escape from this bastard,* I often thought, *what kind of life will be waiting for me in the real world? After this mess is over, who will really be there to love me?* The answers to those questions sometimes made me want to curl up, fall through the floor, and vanish forever.

*If I was dead or alive, you wouldn't care as long as you
fucked over my life and not yours. To hurt someone is not
going to help the situation or the destructive path that you
are taking … My life is too precious for you to think you can
hold me captive like my life is worthless, to live to destroy all
my hopes and dreams, then take what pieces of my heart that
I had left and toss into the trash like yesterday's garbage,
along with everything that I held close to my heart. It's gone,
and I hope that I can get back everything that I lost in life.
I try to hide the hate that burns inside of me … I know it's
wrong to think evil, but I live in a world surrounded by evil
people and I can't help the way I feel inside. If you went
through what I went through, then you might just know how
I feel … Being treated like trash, that will never change, and
I'll never be the same.*

OVER THE NEXT few weeks in our room Gina and I spent a
lot of time whispering about one thing: What was the dude
saying to Amanda when he was with her? When he took her
to his cubbyhole, sometimes I heard him laughing on the
way down the stairs, like he was having a good time. And
when we were all in the kitchen, he would find a way to be
with her separately, even while he kept an eye on Gina and
me. If we all sat down at the table to eat, he would sit next to
her at the other end. It almost seemed like he was trying to
chill with her and enjoy her company. His behavior creeped
me out and made me worry about what he was planning.

# 20

## Hard Labor

*I know somewhere out there, life can be beautiful and there is someone who cares about you. We just have to wait for all the black and gray clouds to go away so we can see the beautiful rain that's behind the clowns that are laughing at us ...*

*I had to taste the bitter sweetness of life and face the pain on my own, then rise and fall. I've got to seize that one moment in time to be free for eternity.*

IN EARLY 2004 a strange thing happened: the dude started saying that Amanda was his wife. I figured that as messed up as he was, in his sick mind, he must think it was true. I didn't spend too much time focusing on what the dude called his "marriage" because it sounded completely ridiculous to me. I kept thinking that if we all ignored the whole thing, it would just fade away. But I couldn't ignore what started to happen next.

Everything changed after the dude claimed that he and Amanda were together. For one thing, he started spending a lot of time downstairs with her. I often heard their two sets of footsteps going down to the main floor. Gina and I could hear him watching cable TV in his room. I had no idea if he still had her chained up or what. On those evenings, when we were all in the kitchen, he had her sit with him, either at the other end of the table or in the living room on the couch, where he could still keep an eye on us.

Around that time the dude started taking me outside a lot more. He would tell me, "You're coming into the backyard to do some work with me." He called it "hard labor," stuff like lifting and moving bricks, cutting wood, and changing the oil on one of his vehicles. Once we got back there, he only made me do those jobs for a little while. Before I knew it, he had me pinned up against the side of his burgundy van. One day he ripped my clothes off and raped me right there in broad daylight.

"Stand still," he whispered, unzipping his jeans. "I'm gonna fuck you real good right now." There were no bushes around the house; anyone passing by could have seen into the backyard if they'd been looking. And after the dude announced that he and Amanda were "married," the rapes outdoors happened way more frequently. This made me wonder if, in his twisted mind, maybe he thought he should try to hide from her all the sex he was still having with me. He kept on raping Gina too, but I felt like he didn't do that nearly as much as he did it to me.

It seemed to me that in his sick mind the dude really thought he and Amanda were a couple. When he was with me he often talked about it. One time, when he had me out on the back porch, he said to me with a straight face: "I called Amanda's mother."

*What?* I felt like throwing up. Not that there was anything in my stomach—I was starving.

"I told her that her daughter is my wife now, that she's okay because she's with me. Then I just hung up." He laughed like that was some kind of a funny joke. "One day," he added, "I'm gonna make you my second wife."

I already knew he was insane, but when he said that, I was sure he must be a demon straight from hell. I wanted to hit him right in the head. I looked down at my feet and cursed him under my breath. Thank God he never brought that up again.

Around that time something else changed in the house: we started getting fewer privileges. The dude had been feeding Gina and me twice a day, but suddenly we were lucky if we got one meal. He stopped giving us alcohol downstairs. Sometimes Gina and I would get just one slice of pizza to share. I eventually got so thin that I could feel my bones; my stomach was always growling. The dude had to tighten my chains because they were practically falling off. I was so starving that I would try to go to sleep, just so I could forget about how hungry I was. Then I'd dream really detailed dreams about food. I'd dream about the kind of fried chicken I had at the Baptist church. I'd imagine that I was having a big piece of chocolate cake. Then I'd wake up to my stomach aching painfully from always being empty. It was awful.

But one change was more terrible than all the other ones: he stopped giving us spiral notebooks.

"You don't deserve it," he told me and Gina one day.

His words felt like a knife slicing right through my heart. I had written on every inch of the notebooks he had already given me; in one of them I drew a skull that had an open mouth, like a dead person who was constantly screaming for help. I felt like I *was* that skull. Desperate for paper, we started writing on the backs of burger wrappers on the floor.

Every now and then he still gave us a couple of sheets of paper, but not an entire notebook. On a lot of days I ran out of places to write down my words, my pictures—my feelings. I couldn't put together letters to my Joey. I couldn't draw my wolves, my butterflies, or my teddy bears. It was like being thrown back down into the basement, where I almost went insane from the terrible fear and boredom. We still had that raggedy TV, but if he got mad at us about anything, he would even take that away for a while. On the last empty page of one of my notebooks I wrote this entry:

> *Behind these concrete walls you let me fall hard. I truly believe no one cares for me. I feel like I'm dying in here. Sometimes I feel powerless to the pain and destruction. I find myself paralyzed. I'm going out of my mind thinking about if I'll ever get home to see my lil' angel. I'm sitting in a prison with no windows and waiting for someone to come rescue me. I'm lying here cold, shivering, but I am still not totally broken.*

One of the hardest parts about this time was that it seemed to me like the dude treated the others better than he did me. Amanda had that good color TV in her room, and sometimes she would talk back to him and say things like, "I don't have to listen to you!" Although I wasn't always in the same room, I never saw him smack her for it. But if I said anything at all to him, I got whacked in the face or stomach. It wasn't like he was *nice* to either of them—far from it! But I felt as if I was the prisoner who got beat down the most. And my perception was that on some days I was the only one he had raped. It was like being on death row.

I knew that wasn't their fault. Only one person can ever be blamed for what happened in that house of horrors—the sick jackass who brought us there in the first place.

In addition to that, over the years that followed, I got pregnant four more times—five in total. Every time, the maniac blamed me for it and made me abort the baby. Every time, I felt like I was dying in my body and my mind.

*Death seems like a quicker solution to my problem … hopefully it don't come to that because I have so much to live for … so much I haven't said and so much I haven't done that I need to accomplish before the end comes … We obey because we have to, not that we want to. This isn't our own life, it's someone else's fantasy world that we are living in. It feels like I'm a prisoner … in the end it was your life to begin with, and you are the one who was wrong, not me … someday I will live my life like it's my last breath.*

ON AN AFTERNOON in the spring of 2006 we all got some horrible news. On our little television set Gina and I heard that Amanda's mother, Louwana, had passed away. The reporter said that Louwana had done everything she could to find Amanda; in 2004 she had even gone on the *Montel Williams Show* and asked a psychic if her daughter was still alive. The psychic told her Amanda was already gone, but in spite of that, Louwana kept looking. I could only imagine the kind of pain she had been in. "She died of heart failure on March 2, 2006," the TV reporter said. All I could think about was that call the dude said he'd made to Louwana. If he really did call her, she must have died from a broken heart.

Later on that day the dude let us out of our chains for a short time. I don't know why he let us walk around freely, but he stayed nearby to watch us. I went over into the room where Amanda was.

"I am so sorry for your loss," I told her.

She stared at me and said, "What?"

That's when I realized she hadn't heard the news on her own television set.

"Your mother just passed away," I said. She began to cry, and I backed out of her door, wanting to give her some peace and quiet. When I was back on my mattress I could hear her sobbing. I felt so terrible for Amanda—and so furious that this man had stolen her from her family.

A few weeks after that I got another surprise. Every morning for a couple of weeks I started hearing Amanda throw up in her room. While we were all downstairs in the kitchen she told us she was nauseous and couldn't keep down any food. Later that evening, when the dude took me into his room, he mentioned how sick Amanda was. "She might be pregnant," he said.

"I imagine she is," I said. "You need to start taking better care of her." If, in his twisted mind, he thought they were married, I felt sure he wouldn't make her abort the baby the way he'd made me.

He looked right at me. "How do you know that?"

I don't know where I got the nerve that night, but I gave him a smart-ass answer. "In a few months you're going to figure it out when there's a baby popping out." He didn't hit me like I thought he would. He smiled—like he was happy there might be a baby on the way.

I was right. Amanda never told me she was pregnant. But she didn't have to—the size of her stomach made it obvious. When she was around five or six months pregnant, her tummy looked like it had a basketball inside. I had so many questions I wanted to ask her: Did she want the child? Was she glad she was pregnant? Was she nervous? Afraid? Excited? Did he ever threaten to beat the baby out of her? But during the whole time she was pregnant Amanda and I said very little to each other—mostly just hi. It seemed the dude was usually lurking around. I could only guess what must have been going through her head. I kept thinking about my babies—the one I was trying to get back to and the ones this monster had killed.

*To My Son: You are my shining star, you are the reason I look forward to a new day. You'll always be in my heart, and that's where you'll always stay. You light the way for me, the day gets hard and I think of you and how we will be together forever. Never apart and one day have a fresh new start with you, because you are my hope to survive.*

# 21

---

# Light of the House

*As I lay down to sleep, I pray the Lord my soul to keep … if I shall die before I wake, I pray the Lord my soul to take, so then all the pain and suffering in life will fade away and I can be free again, so I don't have to dream of faraway places that I will never see, or a love that I will never know, or a family I always wanted but never got, or a son who I will never get to hold and say I love you to. … I pray and hope to keep my son safe and give him a better life than I had, filled with love, happiness, and serenity. I can really use a prayer right now … seems just yesterday I was holding you in my arms, now all those days are gone. I have to keep moving on, I have to look for a bright day at the end of the road.*

In the middle of the night on Christmas Eve, 2006, I felt a tap on my shoulder.

"Get up," a voice said. I rubbed my eyes and sat up on the mattress. At my side Gina was still asleep. "Amanda's been in labor all day," the dude said, unlocking me. "I need you to come down to the basement and help me bring something upstairs." I was out of it. Christmas was a day I had started to hate even more than I used to love it. All those memories of celebrating with Joey had been replaced by ugly ones. On Christmas Eve the radio played one holiday song after another. I could barely keep myself from bawling. I had decided I would do my best to just sleep the day away—and then the dude woke me up. The two of us went downstairs.

Down in the basement there was a small swimming pool. It wasn't the inflatable kind; it was one of those plastic ones that had walls. "Help me get this upstairs," he said. "She's gotta sit in this so she won't mess up the mattress."

I didn't want to help. What I wanted to do was get into my bed and fall back asleep. But I didn't have a choice.

The two of us dragged the plastic pool into Amanda's room. I could tell she was in extreme pain. We put the pool down on the mattress, and he rushed her to get in. I gave Amanda my sweater to wrap around herself—it was very cold in her room. I then took her arm and helped her step over the side and into the pool. Once she got in there, she laid down. The dude stood there, giving me threats. "If this baby doesn't come out alive," he told me, "I'm going to kill you."

I tried to ignore him so I could focus on trying to help Amanda. The dude was no help; he had no idea what to do.

"Push hard, Amanda!" I said.

When her beautiful baby girl finally arrived, I immediately knew there was a problem: her little face was blue. She wasn't breathing.

"You'd better get her breathing!" the dude screamed at me.

My hands trembled and my mind raced. *God, what should I do? How do I bring this baby back to life?* I put a damp rag on the mattress and laid the baby down on it. I then tilted her head up a little bit and pressed on her chest several times. In between that, I breathed into her mouth.

A minute or so later she started screaming. "Aaaaah! Aaaaah! Aaaagh!" It was the sweetest sound I ever heard in that house. The dude snatched the baby from me and took her downstairs, I guess to clean her up.

When it was all over I was exhausted, totally wiped out. I helped Amanda get cleaned up and started to walk back to my room so I could lie down. As soon as I joined Gina on our mattress, the dude came in.

"You're gonna help me get this pool outta here," he said. While Amanda held her newborn, he and I carried the pool downstairs and into the backyard and dumped out the blood. Then I dragged myself back up the stairs and got into bed. It must have been five o'clock in the morning. That was how my Christmas of 2006 began.

I FINALLY GOT to hold the baby that evening. The dude came into my room and handed her to me. Amanda was resting in her room.

"Here she is," he said. He had a big smile on his face. The baby was wrapped in an old raggedy blanket, something he must have pulled out from the back of his closet.

She yawned and looked up at me. "She's so cute!" I said. She was the tiniest little baby I had ever seen. I'm guessing she was five pounds, and maybe even less. She smelled so new and clean—the exact opposite of the dirty house we were in. Gina cooed over her too.

I looked down at her round face and bright eyes. That's when my own eyes started filling up with tears. I missed my Joey so much in that moment. Right then he took the baby away from me and walked back to Amanda's room. All through that night we could hear that little girl crying. I hoped someone would hear her screams and wonder why the sound of a baby was coming from the house of a single man. Gina and I thought that maybe this child would be our way out.

During the next week the dude let Gina and me go into Amanda's room to see her a few different times. Amanda looked worn out. She and the baby were usually curled up together on the mattress, because there was no crib.

"What are you gonna name her?" Gina asked.

"I don't know," Amanda said. She looked down at the baby in her arms. We all started throwing out names.

"I like Jocelyn," Amanda finally said. So that settled it: her new angel would be called Jocelyn. Her middle name was Jade. The dude went to a store and brought home a pink pillow with some kind of duck or chicken on it. He made Amanda write "Jocelyn Castro" on the pillow's tag. Just seeing his last name on there made me gag. I heard Amanda tell the dude that she wanted the baby to have her last name.

"She can be Jocelyn Jade Berry," she said.

*I was right,* I thought. Amanda would never be the "wife" of that idiot. She was just trying to outsmart him.

"Well, she can be 'Berry' inside the house," the dude told Amanda. "But I don't want nobody wondering who 'Berry' is. So outside of here she's 'Castro.'"

*Outside of the house?* That was my first clue that he planned to take his little girl into the real world. Didn't he think his family might catch onto his double life? But then again, the dude didn't do a whole lot of thinking.

After Jocelyn was born he gave them our room, the white one, because it was bigger. "She needs more space for her and the baby," he said.

He moved Gina and me into the pink room, which was connected to the white room. The same pink room where he'd strung me up on those two poles the day he kidnapped me. I could open the door between the two rooms and hear a lot more of what was going on with Amanda and Jocelyn. In fact, the room was so small that I could reach over and push open the connecting door, even when I was on my mattress with my chains on.

I didn't give a rat's ass where he moved me. All the rooms were a dump. But in the pink room things did get a little better. He went back to feeding Gina and me a couple of times a day, and he finally gave me another spiral notebook. And for at least a few weeks after Jocelyn got there he left me alone. I think the new baby distracted him. Even before Jocelyn was old enough to know where she was, she was already bringing some light into our lives.

Not long after Jocelyn was born, the dude let Amanda out of her chains. "I don't want the baby to see you with those on," I heard him tell her. She still couldn't get out of her room: he locked her door, and ours. But at least she didn't have to sit on top of that dingy mattress all day. She could walk around with Jocelyn or play with her in any part of the room.

I loved Jocelyn from the moment I first saw her; she was precious. But I didn't really get to hold her that much. The dude saw me as lower than dirt. He called me worthless in front of Amanda and Gina. He spit in my face. Over and over he reminded everyone that no one in my family was looking for me. And after all that, then he'd yell at me and say, "What's wrong with you? You're supposed to be happy!" I knew he wanted to make me *not* be me. I didn't believe the things he said about me, because that would be letting the darkness win.

But that didn't stop me from adoring Jocelyn. When we were down in the kitchen together in the evenings, my job was to hold her and keep her quiet while Gina cooked and the dude talked to Amanda. I rocked her back and forth and sang her the same songs I used to sing to Joey. I bounced her up and down on my knee. She was such a good baby. Unless she was wet or hungry, she really didn't cry a lot.

In my room I began making some clothes for Jocelyn. She had a couple of outfits, but they were stained and faded. So Gina and I tore up some of our old T-shirts, and then we used a needle and thread the dude gave us to make the baby a few outfits. We sewed some pants, some cute little bootie socks, and a long-sleeved T-shirt. Amanda seemed to love them, but when the dude saw them he said, "Those are ugly."

"Well, it's cold outside!" I said. "This baby needs more clothes!"

"Then I'll buy her some more clothes," he told me. "Stop making her that crap." He was such a selfish bastard. On one hand, I loved having Jocelyn in the house. It gave me something else to think about besides my agony. It brought me joy in the middle of a darkness that felt like it would never end. But on the other hand, I was very sad for her. When you're born into slavery, what kind of life can you really have? So it was a big blessing for us but a huge curse for her, all at the same time. I dreamed that one day that innocent little girl could be free.

I dreamed the same thing for all four of us. I kept seeing Joey's face in my mind, and that's what kept me alive. I couldn't leave him alone on this earth without him knowing me. I kept hearing his little voice in my mind, saying, "Mommy, I need you." That helped me have the strength to go on when I felt like giving up.

Most nights I'd fall asleep praying.

*Dear God ... I will not let this tragedy bring me to my knees or define me all my life. I've got the right path in my sight. I don't want to live forever feeling this pain all over again. I just wish it will go away and never come back.*

*What doesn't kill me can only make me stronger in my heart. Death may seem like an easy solution, but I think surviving with my head held high is better than lying with my head hung low. I'm staring out of the window of pain waiting for my perfect ending ... many days feel like miles of torture in my broken heart. Do you feel my pain ...*

# 22

---

# Juju & Chelsea

*Why must I go through so much pain just to get back to you?*
*My heart fills with so much hate that tears me down ... I*
*just hope to be me again, to live so free.*

*This is for all the women who were told they were nothing*
*... don't let them tear you down or destroy your heart. You*
*are somebody, don't let them tell you any different ... I really*
*deserve to smile even if the pain is too unbearable.*

When you're locked up, time does something funny—it
seems to stop. One way I could tell the days were still passing
was by watching Jocelyn. Almost overnight she grew from a
tiny bundle into the cutest toddler. The dude never kept her
in chains. That's why she could sometimes waddle back and
forth between the pink room and the white one.

"Hey, sweetie!" I would say when I saw her come through
the connecting door. She smiled a lot. She always had on a
cloth diaper. Sometimes it was sagging a little because she
had peed in it.

"How you doin' today?" I'd say, scooping her up into my arms. After Gina and I were moved into the pink room, I got to hold her a lot more, especially when Amanda was downstairs either in the dude's room or taking a shower. By then, as I said earlier, he had started letting us shower once a week. That felt like a luxury after having only one shower during my whole first year in the house.

Jocelyn was around one year old when she began making sounds like she was trying to talk. By the time she was one and a half, she was saying short words, like "Mama!" So the dude came into our room one day and told us, "I'm gonna give you different names—I don't want her to know your real names." Gina and I looked at each other.

"Well, I'm not using any name you give me," I told him. "I'll pick one myself—I'll be Lee." That was Joey's middle name.

"Choose something else, 'cause that's got to do with my kids," he told me. I guess one of his children had "Lee" somewhere in their name.

"How about Angel?" I said.

He gave me a mean look. "You definitely don't look like no angel," he told me.

"Well, then, I'll just call myself Juju," I said. I picked that name because I always loved Jujubes candy.

"Fine," he said. He turned to Gina. "So what's your name gonna be?"

She shrugged, and I gave her a couple of ideas. "How about Hazel?" I said. "Or Chelsea?"

"I like Chelsea," said Gina. So from that day forward, whenever Jocelyn was around, we could only use our fake names: Juju and Chelsea.

In 2009, when Jocelyn was about two, a miracle happened: the dude unlocked Gina and me. He didn't do it out of the kindness of his heart. It was because Jocelyn was getting old enough to understand what was happening around her. She would come up to the side of my and Gina's bed and point at our chains. Sometimes she even pulled at them.

"Juju lock?" she would try to say.

"Get her out of there!" the dude would yell if he saw her touching the chains. "That's not good for her to see." He cared more about his little girl seeing those chains than he did about having locked us up in them.

Around that time he started to take us downstairs more often. On the weekends he sometimes let us stay in the kitchen or the living room for a few hours.

"I can trust you more now," he told us. I went back to thinking about some ways we could try to get out.

I talked to Gina about it. "Maybe we can get out of the back door when he and Amanda are on the couch talking," I said.

She looked at me but didn't answer. That's because both of us knew the truth: he had a gun, and if we tried to run, he wouldn't hesitate to use it. And even if we did get out, he would murder Amanda and Jocelyn. The only way our plan might work was if we were all in it together.

Sometimes the dude would leave our bedroom doors unlocked, but that was just another one of his tests. Not even a minute after he left he would sneak back upstairs and stick his head in the door. He usually didn't say a word; he'd just look to see if any one of us had moved an inch. Every now and then he would throw out another one of his threats: "If you show me that I can't trust you, you'll pay for it."

He kept his gun on his hip most of the time, but to be honest with you, he really didn't have to. By 2008 we were trained. After years of being in prison a crazy thing starts to happen: the locks move from off of your wrists and your ankles and up to your brain. Did I still want to get the hell out of his dungeon so I could reunite with my Joey? Not a day passed that I didn't think about that. At the time I had been there for more than six years. But after you've been raped, humiliated, beaten, and chained for so long, you get into the habit of doing what you're told. Your spirit starts crumbling. You start not to be able to imagine anything different. And it feels like your captor is all-seeing and all-knowing.

*With my wings out wide I'm ready to fly … when I close my eyes, all I want to see is you … When will our dreams become real so we can live our lives out loud, instead of in the dark where we don't belong?*

"Oooh, I just love her big ass," the dude said with a nasty leer.

All of us, including the baby, were in the living room with him. He made us gather around to watch one of his favorite shows, *Keeping Up with the Kardashians.* Kim Kardashian was on the screen. "I wish I could just bend that girl over and do it to her right now," he said.

I had gotten so used to hearing all of the foul things he said that I didn't even look up. Jocelyn, who was almost three by then, was running around the living room and giggling.

After the show was over, the dude made me massage his back.

"I'm sore," he told me. Around that time he had started to ask me to massage him on a lot of nights. *Yuck.* When I was pressing my hands into his back, the cell phone rang. The dude answered and said something in Spanish. He then hung up real quick. "It was that woman again," he said, as if we cared.

All week the dude had been telling us that he'd met some woman at a nightclub. I guess he thought she was hot. "I don't know why she keeps calling here," he added.

The phone rang again. The dude answered and said something else in Spanish. He seemed pissed off. Then he handed the phone to Amanda. "Tell her to stop calling here." He glared at her threateningly. Amanda stared at him for a moment and then did as she was told. He yanked the phone out of her hands and hung up.

My mind raced. *Would I have had the nerve to beg the woman to call 911 with the dude standing right there?* I wasn't sure. I flopped down on the couch, and a tear rolled down my cheek. "Juju mad?" Jocelyn asked when she saw me crying. I wasn't mad—just horribly frustrated that we were so trapped.

A moment later the dude forced me get behind him again and keep massaging. I dug my fingertips into his skin, but I really wanted to wrap my hands around his neck and strangle him to death.

Later on in the room Gina and I whispered about what happened. One thing had become very clear to me: if I was ever going to break out of this prison, I would have to do it myself.

*Vibrant butterfly full of life, every time I see one it reminds me of how precious life can truly be, to be able to fly so free ... wherever she pleases with no cares in the world. I wait for that special moment in time when I get to live my life freely too. No more worries, pain or tears, just happiness and laughter ... One special day I'll get to live my life just like that butterfly and no longer feeling blue inside.*

# 23

# Mustard

*God is not ready for me yet. What do I do when my
world is crumbling down and everything that surrounds
me disappears along with love that turns into hate ...
everything that I once did, I can't do anymore because my
insides are torn from the body.*

When Jocelyn was around two and a half or three, the dude
began taking her out of the house. He also began going to
church every Sunday. I think he was Catholic—that, or Pen-
tecostal, which were the two kind of churches I heard him
mention.

"I've gotta put some religion in my daughter's life," he
told me one afternoon. "She's gotta know about God." A little while before that, the hypocrite had been thrusting himself inside of me. *Whatever, prick.*

Sunday was the one day a week that he bathed—that was
when I heard the pipes rattling in the bathroom. The dude
liked to show Jocelyn off. He seemed happy to have another
child back in his house and in his life. "My family got taken

away from me," he often told me, "and now I have a new one." In his crazy mind he thought he was a good parent. That was one of the reasons he took Jocelyn to church. I guess he thought it was safe for people to meet her, because no one was looking for her. There was no record of her birth; the world didn't know she existed.

The dude also had the nerve to introduce Jocelyn to his band. If you ask me, that was another stupid move—kind of like when he brought his little grandson upstairs. "I'm gonna take Jocelyn down and let her meet the guys," I overheard him tell Amanda one Saturday. At the time I didn't know how he explained where Jocelyn came from. Years later in a news report I read that he told people Jocelyn was the daughter of his girlfriend. Maybe those people believed him. Maybe they didn't. Even if they suspected something fishy, they never called the cops to have it checked out.

Just like us, Jocelyn was kept inside most of the time. The only difference was that she was free to run up and down the stairs on her own, if the dude was at home. When he got back from work he unlocked Amanda's door.

"I'm gonna take her downstairs for a while," he said. I don't know what they did down there—it sounded like he was sometimes watching cartoons with her. My greatest fear was that after she got older he would start to mess with her the same way he did the rest of us.

As Jocelyn grew, I felt more and more protective of her. Losing Joey was one of the most difficult things I ever went through—and spending time with Jocelyn took away some of my heartache. The two of us had so much fun. The dude had bought her all kinds of games and toys. She even had an Xbox and a DVD player so she could watch children's videos.

I got to see her for about an hour a day, usually when the dude was at work. When she was allowed to, Jocelyn would come sit in my room and color.

"Look, Juju!" she would say, pointing to a picture in her coloring book. She colored the same way Joey did, with crayon marks all over the page.

"That's so pretty!" I would tell her. One time I helped her draw a picture of Hello Kitty. I drew it first, and then she tried to copy it. "You did a great job!" I told her. She gave me a huge smile. "You're such a big girl now!"

Using tape, I put her pictures up on my wall, right next to the row of cards I had drawn to celebrate Joey's birthdays. One of my walls was filled with pictures. Sometimes, if the dude was in a pissed-off mood, he would come in there and rip my stuff down. I always started over and put it all back up.

For the most part the dude tried to hide his abuse of us from his daughter. I don't think he wanted her to see him as the evil man he was. But there were times when he hit me in front of her. One evening we were all down in the kitchen. Amanda and Gina were making our usual rice and beans, and Amanda was mashing some up to feed to Jocelyn.

"You fucking bitch!" he screamed at me. He slapped me across my cheek with the back of his huge hand. Gina and Amanda both froze. I don't remember what I'd done to upset him—it never took much to tick him off.

Jocelyn, who was playing by herself in a corner of the kitchen, looked over at us. She didn't make a move. She must have been trying to figure out why her father was so mean to her Auntie Juju.

Once, Jocelyn woke up screaming in the middle of the night. She had had a very bad dream. She was screaming loud enough to wake up the whole neighborhood. The dude came running up the stairs and into her room; the door between our rooms was open that night, so I could see everything that was happening.

"Shut her up!" he yelled at Amanda. Amanda tried to quiet her down by rocking her back and forth and rubbing her back, but Jocelyn kept on sobbing. So the dude put his whole hand over her mouth and nose. "Be quiet!" he told her.

*Is he going to hurt her?* I thought. I wanted to punch the piss out of him. I could tell Amanda was upset too, just by the angry look on her face. Jocelyn eventually calmed down, at least until the next time she had a nightmare. Sometimes when she woke up yelling I tried to help Amanda out by singing to Jocelyn; none of us wanted the dude to come upstairs and touch that child again.

After one of her dreams Jocelyn told me, "The bad man was trying to hurt people."

"It's okay," I told her. "Everything will be fine." The dude may not have hit his own daughter, but the wounds he gave her still seemed very deep.

*

IN THE SUMMER of 2012 Gina started itching. A lot. She got a bunch of little red dots all over her body. "What do you think this is?" she asked me, scratching one of the spots on her arm.

"It could be the chicken pox," I told her. Whatever it was, it was tearing her skin up. The dude didn't seem to care, but the next day he bought her some cream that was supposed to stop the itching. It didn't work.

Over the next several days she got more and more red spots, but I noticed they didn't seem to be turning into poxes. They looked more like mosquito bites. One afternoon I figured it out.

"It isn't chicken pox," I told Gina and the dude. "It's bedbugs." I had just seen one of the little suckers crawl across our mattress. I picked it up and held it right in his face.

"Holy shit!" he said. "You're right. We better close the door so they don't get over into Amanda and Jocelyn's room."

That's what happens when you're a dirt bag; you bring bedbugs into the house. The dude didn't get our mattress from the store. He once told me that he got it from an alley outdoors. "A mattress is just a place to lay down on," he said. "Who cares if it has a few stains on it?"

But by the time 2012 rolled around, that bed didn't just have "a few stains." It was filled with everything from dust and semen to spit and blood. The mattresses were so filthy that I'm surprised we didn't have bedbugs many years before. And when the dude closed off the doors to our room it was a hundred degrees outside—hot as hell, with no ventilation. Gina and I sweated like pigs. But even after I showed him that bug, he didn't throw out that bed. Instead, he came into the room with a huge piece of plastic.

"Get up," he said. He threw the plastic over the mattress. "Well," he told us, "I hope they die."

*I hope you do too!* I thought. A few days later I started getting the bites. I knew that would happen; there's no way you can sleep on top of a mattress filled with bugs and not get eaten alive. Eventually we were both covered with dots from head to toe. Sometimes it would seem like the bites were clearing up. But whenever they started to go away, we'd get a whole bunch of new ones. It was exactly like our experience in the house: just when we thought things were getting a little better, they actually got worse. A new catastrophe was always just around the corner.

We spent the entire miserable summer switching between scratching our bedbug bites and trying to stay cool. Only one good thing happened that whole summer. While we were down in the kitchen the dude let Gina look through a newspaper. In one of the ads she saw a dress she thought I would like. Later, when I wasn't around, she begged the dude to buy it using the money she had "earned"—that big stash of bills he was always throwing at us like we were his little hookers. I couldn't believe he went out and bought the dress, but he did. She later told me the whole story. It was the one and only time he let us "buy" something with "our money."

When Gina surprised me with it, I was so excited. "It's beautiful!" I told her. "I love it!"

It was a sleeveless sundress that had a variety of pretty colors in it—pink, green, and blue. It was so long that it went down way past my ankles. I wore the dress a lot, right on top of all those terrible bedbug bites.

The long, hot days slowly got cooler and shorter, but the daily rapes didn't slow down. Sometimes I tried to zone out by thinking up some way to escape. And I told Gina, "We should start doing exercises so we can get stronger and knock his ass out."

She laughed. But a few days after I said that, we started up a routine. Every morning we got onto the floor and did a bunch of sit-ups and push-ups, even though I felt pretty weak.

"We have to build up enough muscle to break out of here," I said in the middle of one of my sit-ups. Gina nodded and kept exercising.

"Heck, yeah," I told her. "We're busting out of this place." We got a little stronger, but we were still chained up on Seymour Avenue.

Around the end of September I couldn't do it anymore. I was nauseous and leaking milk, pregnant again for the fifth time since I'd been held captive.

THAT FALL, WHEN Jocelyn was five, the dude took her to some kind of outdoor fair or carnival. They returned with some food.

"Jocelyn wanted to get each one of you guys a hot dog," he said. The only trouble was that the hot dog was smothered in mustard—and I am extremely allergic to mustard.

When I was eight years old I ate some deviled eggs. Fifteen minutes later my whole face swelled up and turned red. I couldn't breathe. My mother rushed me to the emergency room. The doctors tested me and discovered that mustard was the cause.

"It could have killed her," the doctor told my mother.

I never ate mustard again. So when the dude came home with a hot dog slathered in it, I knew how dangerous it was for me. He knew it too: whenever he got burgers at McDonald's, I wouldn't eat it if he'd forgotten to ask them to hold the mustard. But now, knowing that I was allergic, he insisted that I eat it anyway. He put the hot dog down on the mattress.

"If you don't eat this," he told me, "you're not getting anything else."

Several days earlier he had gone back to basically starving me. "I'll teach you to do what I tell you to do," he'd said. He stopped taking me downstairs for dinner. Around that time he also figured out that I was pregnant, because I'd started throwing up—so that gave him a good reason to starve me.

"If I have anything to do with it," he told me, "you will never have a baby in this house."

On top of all that, I felt like I was coming down with some kind of virus or head cold. I had been coughing and sneezing nonstop. And my stomach was aching from not having anything to eat. So even though I knew mustard could seriously hurt me, I was tempted to eat the hot dog. Initially I hadn't been able to keep anything down because of the nausea, but as I got a little farther into my pregnancy, my appetite came back. By this point I was so hungry that I thought, *Maybe if I wipe off the mustard, I'll be okay.* Trust me, you think about doing a lot of crazy things when you're dying of hunger, especially if you have no idea whether another meal is coming.

"Eat this or I'll shoot you!" he ordered. If I was going to die either way, I figured I should at least die with a full stomach. So I picked up the hot dog and used the bottom edge of my T-shirt to wipe off the glob of yellow mustard. I put the hot dog up to my mouth, took a bite—and then I held my breath.

Within several minutes my face puffed up. My throat closed. My belly felt like it was being ripped out. "You look really bad," Gina said.

The dude didn't care. He wasn't about to take me to the hospital. He just shrugged. "You'll get over it," he said and walked out of our room.

That night I lay on my mattress and prayed that the mustard would work its way out of my body. "If you're listening, God," I whispered, "I need you to help me right now." But I got worse. Much worse. The next morning my face was twice as puffed up as it was the day before. My whole body had turned the color of a ripe tomato. I couldn't feel my throat or my tongue. When Gina woke up and looked at me, I could see the fear in her eyes.

"Oh my God, what should we do?" she asked. I didn't even have the energy to answer her.

By day two, the way I looked and sounded finally freaked out the dude. Not only was my face huge, but I was also coughing up a bunch of mucus. He brought in a big bottle of cough syrup.

"Take some of this," he said, flinging the bottle down on the bed.

Over the next few days I drank that bottle. It helped my cough a little, but it did nothing for the other symptoms. The dude brought in some black beans from a can, plus some water. Gina mashed it up and fed me. I couldn't get my mouth open wide enough to drink out of the cup, so she used a straw to give me some water.

By the fifth day I couldn't move my body, much less open my mouth. I was in more pain than I had ever been in.

"I can't deal with this anymore," I said softly to Gina. I was losing my desire to fight.

She scooted over to my side of the mattress and cradled my head in her lap. "Michelle, you've gotta stay strong for

Joey," she whispered. "Your son loves you. He needs you. You can't go like this. Please."

One part of me wanted to keep going, but an even bigger part of me just wanted to go ahead and die. How can I keep living this way? If I get through this, will I ever even get back to Joey? Will dying at least put me out of this misery? That's the last thing I remember thinking before everything went black.

What happened next still makes me tremble when I talk about it. Right after that total darkness, I opened my eyes to see a white light. It was brighter than any light I have ever seen here on earth. Then, suddenly, I heard a deep voice. "It's not your time, Michelle," the voice said. "It's not your time. It's not your time." My whole body felt lighter than a feather. The next thing I knew, I heard another voice. This time, it was Gina.

"Stay with me," Gina said. "You can get through this. I know you can. Joey loves you. I love you too."

I opened my eyes to see I was still in that house. Still on that dirty mattress. Still stuck in the life that had led me to the doorway of death. I had crossed over to the other side—I know I did. What I saw and heard isn't something you can just imagine.

A thousand different times in my life I had asked God to show up for me. Like when the man in my family first started abusing me. When I was shivering under that bridge. When the dude strung me up in that pink room. I have never been totally sure if God could hear me or if he even cared. But the voice I heard that night convinced me of one thing: God is real. Definitely. I don't know why he let so many awful things happen in my life. I might never have an answer to that question, and I still get angry sometimes when I think about it. But there is only one way I can explain why I didn't completely kick the bucket that night—God brought me back. I saw it. I heard it. I felt it. And for the rest of my life I will never doubt it.

It took another five days for all my swelling to go away. The whole time Gina stayed right there with me. She fed me some more. She wiped the sweat off my forehead with the palm of her hand. She encouraged me to keep on going. Sometimes God shows up as a deep voice and a bright light. Other times he shows up as a friend named Gina. On a dark night in 2012 God showed up as both.

# 24

## Broken

*You make my head fill with agony and pain from all the*
*things that you pounded in my brain. I have a story that*
*needs to be told. I can see you crystal clear and everything*
*you stole ... the devil just reaps your soul.*

The dude's alarm clock went off every morning as usual, but
around November 2012 I stopped hearing him get out of
bed. He still made his way upstairs with bits and pieces of
crappy food, but he showed up a few hours later than he
always had before. And he wasn't dressed in his bus driver
uniform. That's how I figured out that he wasn't working. He
had been around the house all day for a week when I heard
him telling Amanda about it.

"You lost your job?" she asked him one afternoon.

"Yep," he told her. "I got fired."

Now that he was home all the time he assaulted me at all
hours of the day and night. As the radio DJs started talking
about the holidays and playing holiday music, I could feel
myself dropping into a depression. Christmas was on the way.

It would be my eleventh Christmas in that prison. Throughout the year I thought of Joey, but at Christmas he took over my brain. I had missed so many years of his life. If I saw him again, I might not even recognize him! By the end of 2012 he was thirteen—a teenager. I wondered if he was as tall as his dad. I wondered if he still went crazy over sports. I wondered whether he even remembered I was his mother. He was probably nothing like the little toddler I last lifted into my arms. I cried for both my children—the one I hadn't seen in over a decade and the one that was now growing in my stomach. By then I was about almost three months pregnant. The dude hadn't been able to starve the baby out of me.

The only good thing about Christmas was Jocelyn's birthday. In December 2012 she was six. I know it might sound crazy, but every year the dude hosted a party for her. It wasn't a regular birthday party with other kids; it was just for the four of us who were trapped in that house. Amanda and Gina put up streamers in the living room and a big banner that said, "Happy Birthday." They blew up a bunch of colorful balloons, and the dude had bought a cake from a store. But we ate the same damn rice and beans. And, of course, he blasted his sucky salsa music.

For some reason the dude wouldn't let me come down and help decorate; he only let me join the party toward the end. I loved Jocelyn and wanted to make her feel special, but I was also feeling so hungry and tired that I could barely make it down the stairs. He finally came up and got me.

"You ain't really part of this," he told me. *So why the heck did you force me to come down here?* I thought. I'm pretty sure it was to taunt me, to remind me of all the birthdays I didn't get to celebrate with Jocy. "Just sit on the steps and watch from here." I flopped down onto the bottom step.

The dude videotaped the party, but he would only allow Jocelyn and Amanda to be seen on the tape. I don't know why he was retarded enough to let Amanda be in the video. For years Amanda's face had been all over the local news, and in the video she was recognizable as the girl who had been snatched while she was leaving Burger King.

"Happy birthday to you," we all sang, "happy birthday to you, happy birthday dear Jocelyn … happy birthday to you!"

Jocelyn looked up at her mother with a huge smile on her face. We clapped. As horrible as I felt inside and out, it was nice to see her happy.

Once the party was over, Amanda, Jocelyn, and Gina went back upstairs.

"You stay down here," the dude told me.

I thought he was about to take me into his cubbyhole or the backyard; I was sure throwing his little party had made him horny. But he pointed toward the basement stairs. "Go ahead," he said. I took a step and he followed me. The hairs on the back of my neck stood up. *What is about to happen?*

When I got to the third step he pushed me from behind. I tumbled forward, all the way down to the bottom of the stairs. When I landed, my stomach hit the edge of a bookcase.

"It's time to deal with this!" he shouted. "I'm gonna fix you so you can never have a kid!" Doubled over with my face to the ground, I could hear his boots on the bottom step. Then he kicked me right in the stomach.

"Stop it!" I yelled at the top of my lungs. "Please don't kill my baby again!"

But he wouldn't stop. He swung his heavy boot right into my midsection again and again. "Before you leave this basement," he screamed, "that baby had better be gone!" He slammed the side of my head with his open hand.

As he pounded back up the stairs, I lay there sobbing. "God, help me!" I cried. "Please help me!" I wrapped my arms around my stomach to try to make the throbbing go away. He'd turned up the salsa music upstairs. My hysterical screams mixed in with the singer's words. As I cried out over and over again, I tried to stand up, but before I could make it to my feet, he returned.

"Shut the fuck up!" he yelled. "If you don't stop screaming, I'm gonna really kill you!" He then grabbed me by the back of my shirt and pulled me up the stairs and then up to my room.

Four days later I started to bleed. The dude came into the room and dragged me downstairs to the bathroom. "You'd better hope that baby is dead," he said. He slammed the bathroom door and left.

I crawled over to the toilet and pulled down my sweatpants. I got myself onto the seat and held my face in my hands. A red flood rushed down into the bowl. I couldn't breathe or speak. I felt like an elephant was sitting on my chest. I had cried so much that my face was numb.

"Hurry up in there!" he shouted. A couple of minutes later something splashed into the water. I stood up and stared into the toilet. I reached down and scooped my baby out of the water. I stood there and sobbed. *Why didn't God and Gina let me die?* I thought. *Death would have felt better than seeing my own child destroyed.* I looked down at the fetus in my hands.

"I'm so sorry this happened to you," I wailed. "I am so sorry. You deserved better than this!"

The dude barged in. "I told you to hurry the hell up!" he said. He looked down at my bloody hands and smacked me across the face hard enough to make me drop the fetus.

"It's your fault," he said. "You aborted my baby. I should go get my gun and blow your head off right now." Then he rushed out and came back with a garbage bag. He picked up the fetus and dropped it into the bag. A few seconds later I heard the back door open.

He didn't let me shower. So when I got back upstairs and saw Gina, I was still a bloody, teary mess. The dude threw a pile of white napkins down on the mattress and blurted out, "Use these to clean yourself up." He then stormed out and locked the door. To this day the sight of white napkins makes me feel sick—they remind me of what I went through.

"Oh my God, what happened?" Gina said, rushing over to my side of the mattress.

I began to cry again. "He made me lose the baby," I finally said through sobs. "It's over, Gina."

She got real quiet. "I know you wanted to keep it," she finally said, hugging me, "but sometimes it just doesn't work out that way."

That evening the two of us lay there, side by side on the mattress, which was still covered in plastic. We stared up at the ceiling in total silence. I could hear her breathing. I'm sure she could hear me breathing too. Some experiences are just too painful to even talk about. This was one of them.

THE SPRING OF 2013 seemed colder than the ones before. On March afternoons, when the dude took me out into the backyard to pin me up against his van, I could feel a chill in the air. One day, when he finished with me, I turned toward the door.

"Hold on," he said. He went over to another part of the yard and picked up a shovel and some gloves. "You're going to help me do some work back here today. I'm putting in a garden."

*A garden? Since when did you start gardening?* I thought. But I knew better than to ask questions. I just stared at him.

"We're going to dig a big hole," he said.

Why would you need a big hole for a garden?

"Let's start digging right over there," he said. He pointed to a grassy area in the back. I put on the gloves and stuck the blade of the shovel into the frozen dirt. The big shovel was so much taller than me that I could hardly hold it up, but I somehow managed to sink it into the ground. *Dig. Dig. Dig.* A little bit at a time, I lifted the dirt and tossed it over to my side.

After a couple of minutes of watching me work, he grabbed another shovel and started digging right next to me. "Make it deeper," he barked at me. So I shoveled. And shoveled. And shoveled. By the second hour sweat was pouring from my armpits. My throat was dry. My wrists ached. The hole was getting deeper and deeper, in spite of the fact that the ground was so hard.

That's when it hit me—this wasn't a garden. This was a grave. This dude was planning to bury someone in his yard! Why else would he need such a huge hole? It was definitely big enough for a body.

"Keep digging, bitch!" he kept telling me. "It's not deep enough yet."

Each time I picked up a load of dirt, my pulse raced faster and faster. *This could really be the end,* I thought. The psycho had already murdered my children. Now he was going to murder me.

After three hours the dude put down his shovel and told me I could stop digging. I peeled off my gloves and wiped away the sweat from my forehead.

"That's it for today," he said, breathing heavily. "Maybe we can finish it up tomorrow." *Tomorrow*—a day I feared I might never live to see. But although he mentioned having me dig some more several times after that, to my relief, he never followed through on it. Maybe it was just another one of his crazy mind games, or maybe he was just biding his time until the ground was less frozen.

*They say time will heal the pain, but I don't think that rules apply here . . . I don't think I'm going to recover from this nightmare.*

# 25

## Found

*You will always be in my heart. I'll always be there for you when you fall, to put you back on the ground and make you strong again. I'll always be there to help you through the journey called life. So when you're feeling like life is over, call me and I'll be there to help you through thick and thin, then you can mend the pieces of your life back together.*

On May 6, 2013, I opened my eyes at around ten o'clock. Gina was already up and drawing in her notebook. We weren't chained on that day; as I mentioned earlier, the dude had threatened us so many times with his gun and beat us up if we did anything he didn't like, that we were pretty much afraid to try to break out. We knew that at any minute he could be hiding in the hallway or downstairs, just waiting to see what we'd done so he could make our lives even more hellish. I felt like for me in particular, he'd use any excuse to punch me in the face or choke me.

"Good morning," I said to Gina as I yawned. I covered my mouth with the back of my hand.

"Hey," Gina answered. She was so focused on whatever she was drawing in her notebook that she didn't look up at me. I grabbed my blue spiral notebook and flipped through it to find the empty pages. There were only a few left. *What should I draw today?* I thought. *Flowers—I'll draw some flowers for my Joey.* I sharpened my pencil and began sketching out a bundle of roses. I imagined they were red. As I drew the petals on a rose, I said, "I don't know why, but I have this funny feeling in my stomach."

Gina laid down her pencil and looked over at me. "Why?" she said. "Do you think you're pregnant again or something?"

"Nah, that's not what I mean," I said. "I don't know why, but there's a pit in my stomach. Maybe it's this heat." It was hot, even though we were only wearing tank tops and shorts. We both went back to drawing.

About an hour later I heard Jocelyn giggling. "Daddy, Daddy!" she yelled out as she ran up and down the stairs. It sounded like she and the dude were playing a game. A few minutes later we heard Jocelyn go into her mother's room.

"Hi, Mommy!" she said. She seemed so full of joy. A moment later I heard Amanda's outer door open. It must have been unlocked because I didn't hear any lock unclicking. At first I thought the dude had come up, but I heard Jocelyn skip back downstairs alone, laughing and singing the whole way.

Gina looked over at me. "Do you mind if I turn on the radio?" she said. I nodded; I wasn't in the mood to hear him having a good time.

"Up next," announced the DJ, "we've got a hit single from the R&B singer Ne-Yo!" A second later one of my favorite songs, "Let Me Love You," filled our bedroom. I began tapping my foot on the floor and softly humming along with the words. Gina started moving her shoulders around to the beat. I motioned for her to turn down the radio a little because I didn't want the dude to catch us listening to a black singer. We both kept drawing and enjoying the music.

Jocelyn came running back up the stairs. She was talking so loud that we could hear her over Ne-Yo. "Mommy," she said, "Daddy went to Mamaw's house!" Mamaw was what Jocelyn called the dude's mother. She had actually met his mother a few times.

*This might be our chance,* I thought. *Or it could just be another test.* A few times before, the dude had told Jocelyn he would be gone all day, knowing she would probably repeat it to us. A few minutes after that, he would unlock our door and stick his head in to give us a creepy grin. "I just wanted to see if I could trust you," he said. I realized that Jocelyn's announcement was probably another trap. And besides that, we didn't hear his van pull out of the driveway. So we stayed right on that bed.

*This is why I had that weird feeling,* I thought. *This was a test that could get us all killed.* Amanda and Jocelyn started playing in their room, and Gina and I sat there minding our own business. Jocelyn ran up and down the stairs a couple of more times, playing, singing, and chatting up a storm. After I finished the bouquet of red roses for my huggy bear, I put down my pencil and notebook.

"I'm kind of bored," I told Gina.

She started searching through the radio stations. She found a song she liked, and I got up and started dancing around the room in my bare feet. I didn't feel too good, but then again, I never felt that good.

Right then we heard Jocelyn come running back into her mother's room. A minute later I heard Amanda's door open. Two sets of footsteps went down the stairs. *The dude must be in his cubbyhole,* I thought. The three of them often chilled downstairs together, and he would usually send Jocelyn up to get Amanda. I kept on dancing.

About fifteen minutes later I suddenly realized something: I didn't hear any voices talking downstairs. Just to be sure, I asked Gina to turn off the radio. She did. The main floor seemed completely silent. *Did the dude take Amanda and Jocelyn somewhere?*

The next thing we knew there was a very loud noise. *Pound! Pound! Pound!* It was coming from the front door of the house. It sounded like someone was trying to break down the door! I nearly crapped in my pants. *This is a bad neighborhood,* I thought. *We must be getting robbed.*

The pounding stopped, and I tiptoed over to the door and reached for the knob. Gina watched me. *Is it locked?* I thought as I slowly turned the knob. It wasn't. I opened it a little ways. Then all of a sudden, we heard a *Boom!*

"Hide!" I hissed to Gina. As fast as I could, I ran over to the radiator and tried to crouch down behind it. I was totally freaked out, imagining some drug dealer or robber breaking into the house, finding us upstairs and murdering us. After everything we'd been through, I didn't want to go like that. I couldn't wedge myself behind the radiator, so I ran over and hid behind the dresser and turned off the light. Gina was breathing hard on the other side of the dresser.

"Shhh," I whispered. The house got very quiet again.

We heard heavy footsteps—two sets of them. *This is it,* I thought. My whole body shook. *They're gonna find us and kill us.* I had been so scared when I heard the noise that I'd left the door halfway open.

My throat got tight. I balled up my fist. *What was that? Who's here?*

"Police!" a woman's voice yelled out. "Police!"

Gina and I couldn't see each other in the dark. "I don't know if it's really the police," I whispered. "Anybody can say that."

I don't know what Gina was thinking, but I knew I wasn't planning to move an inch until I found out what was happening.

As the steps got closer I heard some sounds from a walkie-talkie. In the pitch-black I crawled over to the door and peeked out. I thought I could make out a dark blue sleeve. *Could it really be the cops?* I wasn't sure. I couldn't tell who it was, and I didn't want to take a chance in case it was someone *pretending* to be a cop to trick us into coming out. We'd been tortured and held captive for so long that in that moment it was hard to imagine being rescued.

Still feeling terrified, I pulled our door closed. "I'm going in here," I whispered to Gina, but I couldn't tell if she heard me. I then crawled through the connecting door into Amanda's bedroom. I hid behind her TV cabinet. The whole time my heart felt like it was pounding out of my chest and right through my T-shirt.

A few seconds later Amanda's door creaked open. Two sets of black boots walked in. "Is anyone in here?" said the same voice I'd heard before. I didn't say a word. I looked up to see a man and a woman in full police uniforms. They each had guns on their hips. The second I saw their silver badges shining in the dark, I came out from my hiding place—and I leaped right into the woman's arms! I wrapped my arms around that policewoman's throat so tight that I almost choked her.

Gina was crying when she came out. She looked over at me, then back at the police, like she couldn't believe what she was seeing. A river of water came pouring out of her eyes.

"Is anyone else up here with you?" asked the guy cop.

"I don't think so," I told him through my trembling lips. I wasn't sure where Amanda and Jocelyn were. I just knew they weren't up on the second floor.

The woman cop tried to put me down, but I clung to her neck. I had to be sure I would make it out of there alive, especially because I had no clue where the dude was or if I was really safe from him.

"Are there any weapons in the house?" asked the guy cop.

"There's a gun someplace," I told him. "But I don't know where it is."

"We're going to search the rest of the house," the female cop told me.

That's when I finally let her put me down. Another male cop in a short-sleeved blue shirt came up the stairs. "Everything's okay now," he told us. I'm sure he could see how scared we still were. "Get your clothes. I'll wait for you right here at the top of the stairs."

We went back into our room and changed out of our T-shirts and shorts; I put on some sweatpants, a pink sweater, and some socks and shoes. My hands shook the whole time, and my head felt like a whirlwind had just gone through it. I was delirious. "Gina, can you believe it?" I said. "We're free!"

She changed out of her sweats and into a white top and some furry pants with cheetah spots. Crying and laughing at the same time, we started gathering up our notebooks. But when the cops came back in to check on us, they told us to leave our journals there.

"We'll grab those for you later," said the guy in the short sleeves. "Let's go downstairs."

He didn't have to tell us twice! We practically ran over to those stairs. With each step I took, I thought about all the years that had gone by since the dude had tricked me up those stairs by promising me a puppy. I thought of the hundreds of days when his dirty boots pounded up there to rape me. I thought of when he threw me down those steps, trying to kill my baby. Some of the most horrible moments of my life had happened on those steps. And now, at age thirty-two, I was walking down them for the very last time.

When I got to the last step I didn't look back. I wanted to get the hell out of that place forever. I had to get back to my Joey. I looked around for Amanda and Jocelyn, but because they weren't downstairs, I assumed they were already with the police.

A police officer opened the front door. I walked through it. It was the first time I had ever been out on the front porch. The sun felt way too bright. After my eyes got used to the light, I glanced down at my arms. They were ghost-white. I looked out to the street. An ambulance was parked in front of the house.

"Come this way," the policeman said.

The back doors of the ambulance were open. Inside I saw Amanda and Jocelyn. *Was she the one who called the cops?* I thought. *Did she call 911? How did the two of them get out? And where was the dude?* I was still so confused about what had happened. Amanda was holding Jocelyn and bawling her eyes out. The cop helped us get into the truck.

"Juju, are you okay?" asked Jocelyn. I nodded my head and started sobbing. Amanda reached toward me and took my hand. She squeezed it. "We're free now!" she cried. "We're going home!"

After Gina got in, we all hugged and cried like babies. Our years in hell were finally over.

A bald guy who looked like Kojak asked me my name.

"I'm Michelle," I whispered. "Michelle Knight."

He then put an oxygen mask on me, and that made my heart suddenly drop ten feet. The paramedics laid me down on a bed and hooked me up to an IV. "She looks very ill," I heard one of them say. "She's very pale." I was the only one who got a mask and an IV. Someone closed the back doors, and we sped off to the sound of the sirens: *Weee-yooo! Weee-yooo! Weee-yooo!* We made it to the hospital in less than two minutes. The paramedics helped the other girls get out.

A medical crew wheeled me into my own room, and doctors and nurses started coming at me from every direction! "I'm going to examine you," one of them said. She reached out and touched my leg—and I pulled it away. I was embarrassed because the hair on my legs was as thick as a bush. I hadn't been able to shave in years—it was gross. When the nurse saw me moving away, she said, "It's okay, sweetie," and rubbed my arm.

Inside the hospital I didn't get to see Gina and Amanda, although I wanted to. Someone said they went home the next day. From what they told me, I was way too sick to leave the hospital that soon. I hadn't felt great that morning in the house, but I had gotten used to feeling horrible. I had no idea I was practically at death's door.

Over the next few days I got every test you can imagine. I cried through most of them. They must have put a dozen different needles in my arms. And I didn't want any of the male doctors or nurses to come near me. I only felt comfortable with women. At one point a nurse asked me to step up on a scale. When I went into the house I had been about 130 pounds. That day I weighed less than 84.

I had a long list of health problems. My jaw was severely injured from the many times the dude punched me in the face. Once he had socked me in the jaw with a barbell— that's why some of my words come out sounding funny. I also had major nerve damage in my arms; they shake all the time. But the worst injury of all was a bacterial infection that was literally eating away at my stomach. It was a miracle that I was sitting in that hospital.

I learned that a whole lot of folks must have been following my story, because dozens of flowers, balloons, and gifts started pouring in. Every counter in my room was overflowing with stuff! After feeling invisible for most of my life, I felt overwhelmed to suddenly have so much attention. But I was very grateful. People who didn't even know me were showing me more love than I had ever felt in my entire life.

Once I was allowed to eat solid food, my first meal was a cheeseburger (no mustard!) from Steak 'n Shake, plus a cheesecake blizzard from Dairy Queen. For once I wanted to taste a hamburger that wasn't rotten. One of the police officers went out and got me the food himself. When I bit into that big fat burger, it was like going to heaven! Some of the juice dripped down my chin. The blizzard was just as good. I hadn't had ice cream in years—it felt so cold going down my throat.

It was explained to me that I would need a lawyer, and some people quickly helped me find one. My lawyer told me that some people from the FBI would interview me on video-tape. The next day, when she took me to meet with the FBI, I was so nervous! *What will I say? How will I explain everything? Will the other girls be there?* But it was just me and them. Two women interviewed me while some other people listened from behind a wall. I couldn't see them, but they could see me. It was very nerve-wracking; I really hate talking to people when there are other people listening in.

The two women asked me a ton of questions about every detail of what happened in the house and what I went through every single year. They had all my notebooks, so I guessed the police had gotten them out of the house. At times I was like, "I don't remember exactly when some of these things happened—some of the dates have run together in my mind. But I do remember what that sicko did to me."

That first conversation lasted for hours, and I had to go back to talk to them over the next couple of days to give them more information. By the end of it I was wiped out.

Both of my brothers, Eddie and Freddie, came to visit me in the hospital. Eddie wasn't able to come up to my room at that time, I think because of some kind of rule about the number of visitors. The second Freddie and I saw each other we both broke down crying. The last time I had seen him he was a teenager—and he had turned into a grown man.

"I missed you, sister!" he said.

"I missed you too!" I said. We hugged each other so tightly.

I was too emotional to talk to him very much. Also, I wasn't ready to have a conversation about our parents. The memories of what I went through when I was a little girl were still too painful. Seeing them would remind me of all that. There was just one person I couldn't wait to see—Joey.

"I'm going to need everyone to just give me some space for awhile," I told Freddie. "I've got to figure out what I'm going to do with myself when I get out of here."

Freddie said that he understood. After a few minutes he hugged me again and then left. On his way out he gave me his cell number. "Whenever you're ready," he said, "call me." I nodded.

That same evening I told the hospital staff that I didn't want to see any more visitors—not even family. My heart couldn't take it. I wanted my privacy and some time to start healing.

"Don't you want to see the rest of your family?" my lawyer asked me several times.

"I don't want to talk about it right now," I told her.

Later on, my lawyer told me that the FBI had found an assisted living home for me. "It's safe for you to stay there until you figure out what you want to do next." She said it was the best thing for me, but I was sad that I didn't have a real home of my own to go back to.

I left the hospital on May 10, 2013—four days after we escaped. I slipped out of there quietly, mostly because I wasn't ready to talk to the media or anyone else. It was too frightening. A driver took me to my new home at the assisted living facility. We drove for at least an hour. As I stared out the window at the city, I was shocked at how much had changed. There were tall buildings I had never seen before. The downtown area had new houses and apartment buildings. Even the city buses looked different; the drivers now sat behind plastic barriers. I sat in the backseat and stared out at the unfamiliar surroundings. For eleven years my life had stood still, but Cleveland and the rest of the world had moved on. All I could do was weep.

# 26

## Starting Over

THE ASSISTED LIVING facility was a two-story house run by a couple. They lived in their own separate area upstairs. Downstairs there were three double rooms, each shared by two people. There were seven or eight people altogether. Thank God I had my own room. And after eleven years locked away on a top floor, at last I got to live on the main floor. One resident was seventy, another was eighty-five, and there was even a ninety-five-year-old. A few months later an eighteen-year-old came, which gave me someone closer to my age to talk to.

But when you've spent eleven years in prison the last thing you're looking for is "assistance" in a group home. What you want is freedom. You want to take control of every little decision that someone else has been dictating—like cooking your own food. I didn't care for the meals they made (mostly Polish food), but there wasn't much I could do about that. And when I first got there the people who ran the place kept trying to clean up for me. I know they were just trying to be helpful, but I really wanted to do it all myself.

Don't get me wrong: I was thrilled and grateful to be safely away from that maniac. Do you have any idea what it's like to wake up and realize that no one is going to rape you that day? How wonderful it is to see the sunlight pouring through your window? How great it is to just walk around without a heavy chain on your wrist or ankle? It feels amazing. And once you have that feeling, you want your full independence. In other words, you want your whole life back.

A couple of days after I got to the house I finally watched some television. OH. MY. GOD. I knew our escape was a big deal—my lawyer had filled me in on some parts of the story—but until I saw the news I didn't realize that the entire *world* was talking about it. I heard that Amanda told police that she realized the dude was gone when she came downstairs; she noticed he had left the inner front door unlocked. The storm door had a chain on it, so it would only open a little. But that crack was big enough for her to stick her arm through it. One reporter said that Amanda started screaming for help and waving. I never heard those screams up in my bedroom, so I wondered if she had been yelling while Gina and I were sitting in the room listening to the radio.

A black guy in the neighborhood, Charles Ramsey, told the cops that he heard the screaming while he was sitting at home, eating some McDonald's. "I come outside," he said in one interview, "and I see this girl going nuts trying to get out of a house. So I got on the porch, and she says, 'Help me, I've been here a long time.' I figured it was a domestic violence dispute."

He and another neighbor, a Spanish guy named Angel Cadero, kicked out the bottom of the storm door. That must have been the pounding Gina and I heard when we thought someone was trying to rob us. Both Charles and Angel as well as the police and rescue people, the doctors and nurses, and everyone else who helped us out that day will always be my heroes.

Here's what else I heard on the news: after Amanda crawled out of the bottom of the front door, she held onto Jocelyn real tight and ran across the street to a neighbor's house. From there she called 911. Just about every news station in Cleveland was replaying the 911 call. This is part of the transcript from that call:

AMANDA: Help me. I'm Amanda Berry.

OPERATOR: You need police, fire, ambulance?

AMANDA: I need police.

OPERATOR: Okay, and what's going on there?

AMANDA: I've been kidnapped and I've been missing for ten years, and I'm, I'm here, I'm free now.

OPERATOR: Okay, and what's your address?

AMANDA: 2207 Seymour Avenue.

OPERATOR: 2207 Seymour. Looks like you're calling me from 2210.

AMANDA: I'm across the street. I'm using the phone.

OPERATOR: Okay, stay there with those neighbors. Talk to police when they get there.

When the cops got to the dude's house Amanda told them Gina and I were still stuck inside. According to a couple of reports I heard, she also told them they could probably find the dude in the neighborhood, driving a blue Mazda Miata convertible. I had never seen that car, but he used it when he drove Jocelyn around.

I will probably never know every detail of what happened on the day of our escape, because I was in my room until the police came upstairs. And I didn't really get to talk to Amanda much after we rode in the back of the ambulance on May 6. Months later I saw her for a couple of minutes when the three of us videotaped a statement for the press. But there were so many people around us that we couldn't really sit down and talk.

From what my lawyer told me, the police found Ariel Castro in a McDonald's parking lot, sitting in his Mazda with one of his brothers, Onil. The police arrested them, and, later, another brother, Pedro. The brothers were let go three days later on May 9 because the police said they didn't have anything to do with our kidnappings. Both of them said they had visited the house on Seymour but that the dude kept them in the kitchen area. They said he was always very secretive, and he kept padlocks on a lot of his doors. They also said they had no clue we were in the house and if they had known, they definitely would have called the cops.

The behavior his brothers described matches what I knew about the dude. No one was more sneaky or manipulative than that monster. His own son, Anthony, said he had no idea what his father had done. He told the press that just a couple of weeks before our escape his father had asked him if he thought Amanda Berry was still alive. When Anthony told his dad that he thought Amanda was gone, the dude said, "Really? You think so?" Anthony thought that was weird at the time, but he had no idea his father actually had Amanda in captivity.

In hindsight I think maybe the dude *wanted* to get caught. His whole world was crumbling; he had lost his job. I could tell he was fed up with his life. Toward the end he would say things like, "One day they're going to find out what I did and lock me away." He knew he wasn't going to be able to keep up his lie for much longer, with Jocelyn getting older. That's probably why he mentioned Amanda to his son. Somewhere inside of him maybe he wanted someone to catch him so the insanity could just be over.

Over the summer of 2013 I followed the news stories. The police charged the dude with four counts of kidnapping and three counts of rape. I thought, *Is that it? Just three?* But on July 26 he pled guilty to 937 crimes, including rape, assault, and murder. *That sounds more like it*, I thought.

As part of that deal he would get life in prison without the chance for parole—and his disgusting house would be destroyed. Some of what he said in court made me furious. He talked about his porn addiction and how he was abused when he was a kid. I had heard it all before. Plenty of people get abused, but they don't go out and kidnap three women. I didn't feel sorry for him; I was still angry.

BEFORE THE DUDE's sentencing hearing on August 1, I had decided I wanted to testify. My lawyers didn't think that was a good idea. I think they wanted to protect me from seeing him again.

"I need to face my demon," I told them. "I want to speak in court. I don't have a problem with doing that."

Several weeks before the hearing Gina and I talked on the phone. "Are you going to testify?" I asked her.

She sighed. "I don't think I'm ready," she told me. "Are you?"

"Heck yeah," I told her. "I don't want to look back later on and wish that I had done it."

Gina did not testify, and for her that was the right choice. Her cousin, Sylvia Colon, gave a comment on behalf of her and her family. My lawyer told me that Amanda wasn't planning to go to court either; her sister, Beth Serrano, would speak for her instead. Each one of us had to pick our own path. I chose to write out a statement and speak, mostly because it felt like a way for me to start healing. Every day in that house that man did the most horrible things to me. I wanted to prove to him and to the world that he might have hurt me very badly, but he hadn't broken me. In the end I was still here. Still standing strong.

On the day of the sentencing I didn't think too much about what I would wear. I just threw on a flowered dress I had. I wasn't focused on what anybody else thought of me or how I would sound. I walked into the courtroom and took my seat next to my lawyers. When I first saw the dude it felt a little creepy. The whole time he sat at a table wearing handcuffs, he kept staring at me. It was like his eyes were saying, "Please tell them I didn't do anything wrong."

I felt disgusted. He looked skinnier than he had in the house. I guess he didn't like the food they were giving him in jail. *Now you know how I felt,* I thought. He was a little bit cleaned up, but he was still as ugly as ever. Especially in that orange jumpsuit.

The family members of Gina and Amanda spoke before I did. When I finally got up to read my statement, my hands were trembling, as usual. But other than that, I felt pretty calm:

*Good afternoon. My name is Michelle Knight. And I would like to tell you what this was like for me. I missed my son every day. I wondered if I was ever going to see him again. He was only two and a half years old when I was taken. I look inside my heart and I see my son. I cried every night. I was so alone. I worried about what would happen to me and the other girls every day. Days never got shorter. Days turned into nights. Nights turned into days. The years turned into eternity.*

*I knew nobody cared about me. He told me that my family didn't care even on holidays. Christmas was the most traumatic day because I never got to spend it with my son. Nobody should ever have to go through what I went through, or anybody else, not even the worst enemy.*

*Gina was my teammate. She never let me fall. I never let her fall. She nursed me back to health when I was dying from his abuse. My friendship with her is the only thing that was good out of this situation. We said we would someday make it out alive, and we did.*

*Ariel Castro, I remember all the times that you came home talking about what everybody else did wrong and act like you wasn't doing the same thing. You said, at least I didn't kill you. But you took eleven years of my life away, and I have got it back. I spent eleven years in hell, and now your hell is just beginning.*

*I will overcome all this that happened, but you will face hell for eternity. From this moment on, I will not let you define me or affect who I am. I will live on. You will die a little every day.*

*As you think about the eleven years and atrocities you inflicted on us, what does God think of you hypocritically going to church every Sunday, coming home to torture us? The death penalty would be so much easier. You don't deserve that. You deserve to spend life in prison. I can forgive you, but I will never forget. With the guidance of God, I will prevail and help others that suffered at the hands of others.*

*Writing this statement gave me the strength to be a stronger woman, and know that there's good. There is more good than evil. I know that there are a lot of people going through hard times, but we need to reach out a hand and hold them and let them know that they're being heard. After eleven years, I am finally being heard, and it's liberating. Thank you all. I love you. God bless you.*

After I got done reading, I felt so free, but it was a different kind of freedom from the kind I got on May 6. Getting out of the house was liberty for my body; showing up in court was freedom for my emotions and spirit. When I sat back down my lawyer and a few other people hugged me, and I cried. I didn't cry because I was sad. Those were tears of happiness and relief.

The dude was allowed to speak during the sentencing. "People are trying to paint me as a monster, and I'm not a monster," he said. "I'm sick."

That last part was the only true thing that came out of his mouth that day. He claimed he wasn't violent. He even had the nerve to say that the sex we had was "consensual" and that there was "harmony" in the house. After it was over I felt like justice was done. The judge gave him the worst sentence he could get: life in prison with no chance for parole, plus a thousand years.

About a month after he was sentenced, the woman who ran my assisted living facility came into my room to talk with me.

"Did you watch the news today?" she asked me. I hadn't. "Well, then I'd better tell you something," she said. "Ariel Castro killed himself today."

I told her I wanted to be alone. Later on, I turned on the news to hear the details: the dude had hanged himself with a bed sheet. I sat there and cried. *What a punk!* I wanted him to sit in his cell and rot away a little bit at a time for the rest of his life, just like he forced me to do.

The next morning I called Gina. She had heard the news, and she told me that she had cried too. She was just as angry as I was that he took the coward's way out.

"He couldn't even deal with one month of the torture that he put us through," I told her.

Several weeks later, when the news came out that he had killed himself by trying something called "auto-erotic asphyxiation" (basically, he used the sheet to choke himself to make his orgasm more intense), I wasn't surprised. I figured he got that idea from that show he used to watch about weird fetishes.

GINA AND I talked on the phone a few times after that day. She was my best friend in that house, the person I was literally chained to. I wanted to talk to her every single day. But as the months went by there were fewer phone calls between us. Just like me, she had to sort out her feelings and make her own decisions. I had to respect her choice to move on. If it wasn't for Gina helping me in that house, I wouldn't be here. For the rest of my life I will be thankful for her friendship.

Not long after I got to the assisted living facility I started seeing a counselor. To be honest, I had a hard time opening up to her about what I was feeling. It's not easy to talk to someone who doesn't know you. Even though she was a very nice woman, she couldn't take the place of Gina. Only two other people in this world have any clue what I went through—Gina and Amanda.

People come up to me on the street all the time and ask, "How are you doing?" I know they mean well. But you can't really explain to someone what it's like to go from sharing a dirty mattress with a friend to suddenly feeling all alone in the world. It's impossible for someone who didn't live through that to get that, even if they really care about you. That's why I just sit and write in my diary and draw a lot. It keeps me sane.

It took several months for the FBI to return my spiral notebooks. I read through every single one of them, all the painful memories. Sometimes I had to stop reading because it was too much. But in a way that's why I needed to read them. In order to get past something terrible, sometimes you have to walk through the pain, not around it. It might be messy. It might make you sob. But if you let yourself cry long enough, you finally reach the bottom of your tears. I haven't reached the bottom yet, but I know that someday I will.

PEOPLE ASK ME all the time where my strength came from during those eleven years in hell. The answer comes down to one word: *Joey*. Gina helped me hold on to hope in my darkest moments, but the hope itself was my son. My huggy bear. My reason for waking up every morning. Since the moment I had to say good-bye to him I have always held him in my heart. The desire to get him back is what has kept me breathing. I'm here today because of him. Sometimes people stay alive for one another. I've stayed alive for Joey.

While I was still in the hospital I had one big question for my lawyer: "How is Joey?"

She cleared her throat, looked directly at me, and spoke softly. "Well," she said, "he was adopted by a wonderful foster family when he was four." I looked down and tried to keep the tears from coming. I was glad he was in good hands, but I wanted to see him so badly.

"Will I ever get to see him again?" I asked.

She paused. "I don't know," she finally said. "We'll have to figure that out."

I couldn't hold back the flood anymore. I held my face in my hands and cried for an hour.

At first that news broke my heart, but I have come to understand it. My lawyer explained to me that my son's adoptive family doesn't want me to be directly in touch with him. They're afraid that might be too unsettling for him, and as much as I want to wrap my arms around him so tightly and share so many things with him, I'm scared of the same thing too. He might have seen the story of my escape on the news, but I don't know if he even realizes I am his mother. In fact, I don't even know if his new family calls him Joey. They might have given him a different name when they adopted him. If I showed up out of nowhere, it could turn his world upside down. I care about him too much to do that.

I told my lawyer that I wanted to write to Joey's adoptive parents. She said that she could pass a letter to them through the FBI. So one evening I sat down and wrote my letter. Here is part of what it said:

To Whom It May Concern:

Thank you for watching over my son while I was gone. It gives me peace of mind knowing my son has been in good hands during the eleven years when I was a hostage. I thought of him often and dreamed about what he looked like as a toddler, his first steps, his first words, his first day of school, his likes and dislikes, and how his personality was developing. I wondered if he liked to sing like me, whether he was shy or talkative, and what he liked to play with. As years passed, I wondered if he liked baseball or football.

I wish I had a photo of him. I would be so
appreciative if you could find it in your heart to
send me a picture of my son as a baby and a little
boy. I know you will always be his parents, and that
won't change. I won't try to take him away. I am just
hoping you can help me fill the hole in my heart with
whatever photos or stories you are willing to share
with me.

My son's family was kind enough to write back. That was
why I was able to sit in my lawyer's office that day and look
through the photos of Joey. Those pictures are a treasure to
me. Each morning I take them out of the safe place where I
keep them and lay them out on the counter. I look at them
and wonder what my son's doing. What made him laugh the
day before. Who his friends are now. I will never get tired of
looking at those pictures. I will also never give up hoping for
a miracle—that I'll be able to hug my child just one more
time.

I don't know if I will ever see Joey again. I miss him more
than you can imagine. At the same time I love him so much
that I don't want to interrupt his life. He has a new family
now. He's in a good environment. I would never rip him out
of his world just so he can be in mine. Sometimes you have
to care about people the way they need you to care about
them. I have to love Joey enough to let him go. And that is
what I've done.

Without Joey, I'm left with just me. A girl who once lived
under a bridge. A young mom who had to drop out of school.
A woman who was locked away for eleven long years. I'm still
trying to figure out where to go from here; on many days I

honestly feel lost. I spend a lot of time asking myself, Can I really be happy without my son? Who was I before I had him? And why did so many awful things happen to me in the first place? I don't have all the answers. I probably never will. But I have realized that my life can't get better if I dwell on everything I've been through. I have to look ahead.

The horrors I survived don't have to define me—and with God's help I'm not going to let them. One day at a time, one breath at a time, I am choosing to move forward. After crawling my way out of a dark bedroom and into a brand new life, that's the best gift I can give myself.

# 27

---

# A Life Reclaimed

WHILE I WAS still living in that assisted living facility, Ariel Castro's "house of horrors" was torn down on August 7, 2013. By then the cops were done with all their searching. Thank God they never found any bodies on the dude's property. They did run across the $22,000 in cash he had stashed in his dryer. The prosecutors offered that money to me, Gina, and Amanda. Every one of us turned it down because we wanted it to be put toward improving the neighborhood. In my eyes that was dirty money, and the only way to clean it up was to use it for something good.

I chose to be there on the early morning when the house was destroyed. "Are you sure you want to be there?" my lawyer asked me.

"Heck yeah," I told her. "I want to go."

I wanted to show up for the same reason I wanted to speak up in court. It was one more way for me to heal. The demolition was scheduled for 7:30 A.M., but I came to the area early so I could hand out yellow balloons to the dozens of people who were standing all along Seymour Avenue.

"Here you go," I said to one woman as I handed her a balloon. "This stands for one of the hundreds of people who are still missing."

Why did I give out the balloons? Because I wanted every mother out there to stay strong and keep hoping. I wanted all the victims who are screaming for help to know we haven't forgotten them. We're listening for their voices—and we will never stop looking for them. That morning I and so many others let our balloons float away up to heaven. It was the most beautiful sight.

Right before the crane tore into the pink room in the upstairs part of the house, I left. I really wanted to stay, but my lawyer wanted to protect me from getting overwhelmed by too many media interviews. As I rode away I thought about all the years I wasted in that house. All the times I'd been abused. All the days I cried because I missed Joey so much. Sometimes, in order to move onto something better, you first have to clear away something bad. That's why that house needed to be demolished. That's also why I'm trying to let go of the memories of the many awful things I survived there.

My house of hope—that's what I call the new place I finally moved into around Thanksgiving of 2013. That's right: I now have my own apartment for the first time! I love it. Seriously. The walls are painted in this light, leafy green color. It's so soothing. It makes me feel like I'm outdoors, which is a great feeling after spending so many years locked inside. There are two huge windows in the living room, and the light comes pouring in every morning. Many times every day I just go stand by the window and take in the sunshine. Then at night I also look up at the moon and stars. I don't think

I'll ever get tired of staring out the window. It's the most amazing view in the world.

The smallest things make me happy in that apartment. For one thing, I get up and make my own coffee every morning. After that I can either read a book or do some paintings—it's *my choice* what I want to do. Lately I've really gotten into watercolors, and I paint a lot of flowers and blue skies. Sometimes, in the afternoon or evening, I watch some TV. And let me tell you something: I can put it on any station I want. Sometimes, if I'm flipping through the channels, and I happen to see a black person on the screen, I let it stay on that channel for a long time—just for the hell of it! It's my little way of flipping off the dude who never let me watch programs with African Americans in them. Some of my favorite shows to watch are *The Vampire Diaries*, any of the CSI shows, and *Dancing with the Stars*. And just like Joey, I love all kinds of sports, especially baseball and basketball. Go, Cleveland Cavs!

In the evenings, right before I go to bed, sometimes I write in my journal. My new one is pink and has the word "Love" on the cover. During the holidays I had a wonderful time with some great new friends that I've met since I left the house. This is what I wrote about my first Christmas in the new apartment: "Today let all of our hearts be light and filled with Christmas joy. I will enjoy my friends. I will give thanks for Joey and pray that he's doing well. I will thank God for His blessings. And I will always remember that the true meaning of Christmas comes from the heart." I exchanged a couple of gifts with my friends, but I already had the greatest gift of all—my freedom. I have my life back again.

Some people ask me if I want to have another child. I love children, but because of the physical damage the dude caused to me, I can't have another child out of my body. But I do want to have children in my life. You don't have to be a biological mom to share your love with a kid who needs you. There are so many hurting and desperate children in our world. So in the next few years I will be looking for ways to offer them love, the kind of love I've always wished I could've gotten more of.

Until then I have another little one to take care of—I finally got a puppy! He's a Chihuahua, and he's the cutest thing. Sometimes seeing him makes me think of my sweet Lobo, and I get a little sad. But he's so full of energy and joy that it's hard to stay depressed when he's around.

WHEN I FIRST escaped from the house I could see right away how much Cleveland had changed, just by riding through it. But since then I've also seen how many other things have changed in the whole country! For one thing, I had never used a smart phone. Someone gave me the gift of an iPhone, and I didn't even know how to turn the dang thing on. Thankfully someone in the assisted living facility showed me how to use it. And don't even get me started on Facebook, Twitter, e-mail, texting, and all the other ways people can stay in touch. In one way it's great. But for me it can get overwhelming. When it does, I just turn everything off and write in my journal, sing (I love anything by Mariah Carey), or paint (red is my favorite color for flowers, and blue is the color that always reminds me of my son).

I missed a lot of stuff while I was in that dungeon: Hurricane Katrina, the tsunami in Asia, the Haiti earthquake, and Hurricane Sandy. Michael Jackson and Whitney Houston both passed away while I was in prison. The whole economy got turned upside down, and a bunch of folks lost their houses and jobs. We got our first African American president. Saddam Hussein was killed. I had heard about some of these things on the radio when I was in the house, but I had never had the chance to talk to people in the outside world about them. So when I got into the assisted living facility I had a lot of catching up to do. The people in that house might have been old, but I did have some good conversations with several of them.

On Saturday nights I really love to go out dancing. A couple of friends go with me. Hip-hop is my favorite. When I'm out there on the dance floor I feel so relaxed. After you've been locked up in chains for eleven years and forced to pee in a bucket, you don't take going out dancing for granted. It's so wonderful to just be able to move around freely. And I love to sing; I'll sing along to songs by Katy Perry, Rihanna, and lots of others.

On Sundays I've started going to church. I've visited a few, and I found one that has slammin' music—maybe I'll even join the choir. But I might go to a couple of more churches before I pick one. I'm also hoping I can find that church I went to when I was homeless. I wonder if Arsenio is still there. I'd love to see him and thank him for being so nice to me way back when I was starving and freezing cold.

Near the end of 2013 one big dream came true for me: I went to Disneyland. When my son was small I really wanted to take him to see Winnie the Pooh, Mickey, and Flower, that little skunk in *Bambi*. After I went on the *Dr. Phil Show* to do an interview, Dr. Phil and his producers were sweet enough to arrange the whole thing for me (Thank you so much, Dr. Phil!). Peggy, my lawyer, flew out to Los Angeles with me. I know it might sound crazy to you, but it was actually the first time I ever flew in a plane.

I was so excited that I packed way too much. "Ma'am, would you please step aside for a moment?" one of the TSA agents asked me when we got to the gate. I had just put my suitcase through the X-ray machine, and I had a huge bottle of water in there. Plus, I had a large tube of toothpaste and a container of mouthwash right on top.

"You can't take these liquids on the plane," the agent told me. "Your liquids have to be 3.4 ounces or less. You'll have to go back and check this bag, or else I'll need to throw these liquids away."

I gave her a puzzled look. "But I didn't know I couldn't have liquids."

She stared at me. "This has been the rule for at least the last ten years," she said.

That's when Peggy cut in: "Well, you have no idea where she's been for the last ten years!"

We both kind of laughed, and the agent probably just thought we were nuts or something. I ended up going all the way back to the check-in counter to check my bag. From now on, I know the rules!

Once we got up into the air I couldn't stop staring out the window. "I feel like I'm close to heaven!" I told Peggy. She shook her head and smiled. I'm sure it was just another trip for a lot of people who were traveling that day. But for me it was a whole new world, one filled with blue skies and the most fluffy clouds I've ever seen (I was so amazed when we flew right through them!). When we landed and rode over to the hotel I was so surprised at how big Los Angeles felt. And there were thousands of cars on their freeways, maybe even millions! I didn't love all that traffic, but you can't beat the weather. It was 75 degrees the whole time I was there. Perfect.

Now that I've seen Mickey (very cool!), I have so many other dreams too. When people see me on the streets, a lot of them come up to me and ask, "So what are you going to do next?" Well, I'm already back in school. In January I started taking cooking classes. For at least two years I'll be stirring up all kinds of foods—Spanish, French, Italian, and, of course, American. So far I really love it.

One day I want to open a restaurant. When you give someone a great meal, it's like giving a little bit of your heart. I hope people from all over the world will come eat what I have to cook.

I want to bless other people as much I've been blessed. Whenever I say that, some people seem surprised that I see my life as a blessing after all the terrible things I went through. But the blessing is that I made it out alive. I'm still here. Still breathing every day. And I'm still able to do something for other people. There is no better blessing than that.

MY FAMILY HAS been one of the hardest things for me to talk about since I escaped from the house. First of all, I never heard anything from my father after I got out. I don't know where he is or if he's still even alive. When it comes to my mother, a lot of people don't understand why I don't want to see her again. Well, once I left the hospital I started following the news. I saw some reports that my mother said I grew up helping her work in a vegetable garden and that I fed apples to a neighbor's pet pony. I was like, *What the heck? Who is she talking about?* That never happened!

Through her lawyer, my mother released this statement: "Michelle, my daughter, has been the victim of long-term and profound and unspeakable torture. Her point of view has been altered by that monster and what he did to her. What I have heard that she said about me breaks my heart. That is because what she now believes, while not true, increases her pain. I love my daughter. I always have and always will. I pray that someday she will heal enough to know that again."

All I can tell you is this: there was a lot of pain in my childhood. But I'm not here to blame my mother or make her feel bad. Now that I'm older I understand that when you've been through a lot of pain yourself, you're just doing your best to get through it. Maybe that's what happened with my mother. Like everyone, I know she has had some difficult times in her life, and I hope everything turns out well for her. But when it comes to us getting back in touch with each other, that's not the best choice for me right now. I need some space to take my life in a new direction.

I really do miss some of the other family members, like my brothers and my cousins Lisa, Deanna, and April. But I'm scared that if I get back in touch with one person in the family, that will lead to getting back in touch with my mother, and I'm not ready to do that. I truly hope that one day she will understand my point of view. But even if she doesn't, I have to look toward the future and try to find some happiness.

And then there's the dude. I think the world expects me to hate him for the rest of my life, and I won't lie: there are still a lot of days when I get very angry about the things he did to me. But a little at a time, I'm learning to let go of the hate. I'm not saying he deserves to be let off the hook for what he did. What I'm saying is that *I* deserve to be free. And I can't have freedom if I'm walking around every day with resentment and bitterness. Forgiveness is the only way I can truly reclaim my life. If I don't forgive him, then it'll be like he imprisoned me twice: first while he held me in his house, and now even after he's gone. I'm letting my hatred of him go so I can truly get my life back.

I don't know why my life has turned out the way it did. I sometimes wonder, What was the point of all this pain I've been through? Why couldn't God make it possible for us to never go through hard things? One day in heaven I'll have to ask him about that. But for now the only kind of sense I can make out of everything that has happened is this: we all go through hard things. We might wish we didn't, but we do. Even if I don't understand my pain, I've got to turn it into some kind of purpose.

When I was on my last breath in that house, God kept me alive for a reason. I believe the reason is so I can help others who have been in my situation. When I'm feeling lost, that's the purpose I hold onto. Becoming a voice for those who can't speak, sharing love with other people around me— that's the only way I've been able to find myself again.

# Afterword

EVER SINCE I GOT OUT of the Cleveland house that I was locked up in for eleven years, one of my biggest goals has been to improve my life. And the publication of *Finding Me* has helped me do that by letting me share my story with people all over the world. Through their e-mails and letters as well as when we talk in person after my speaking engagements, connecting with people who've read my book has been a gift I have really loved. Your support has meant so much to me, and wherever I go I feel the love of so many who are rooting for me.

Of course when I do my talks I discuss all those years that I spent in the "House of Horrors." But in my private life I try not to dwell on it or let it control me. I want to turn my experiences into something that gives hope to other people who are going through traumatic events in their lives. I would say that my biggest goal is to help other survivors get past their fears and to turn them into strengths. Believe me—I know how crippling those fears can be; I have to live with them every day. But nothing makes me happier than hearing from someone who's read my book or heard me speak, telling me that I've helped them get through whatever difficult things they're dealing with.

As I mentioned in an earlier chapter, I have also really enjoyed going to culinary school and learning to cook. After

not being able to make my own food for so long, I love finding a new recipe and trying it out and, especially, feeding
my friends. The look on their faces when my dish hits the
spot makes me so happy. I've also been writing songs and
recording them, which feeds my soul and gives me a sense of
inner peace. I've set up a painting studio in my new home,
and every day I try to paint a little bit. But the thing I'm
most excited about recently is taking boxing lessons. I like to
watch the matches on TV, and in addition to my love of the
sport, it's great exercise and makes me feel strong. In fact, at
some point I hope to cross off a big item on my bucket list:
compete in an actual boxing match.

One year ago I barely had time to leave my apartment with
all the work I had to do, working on *Finding Me*. Since then
I've left that apartment in the dust to go on a month-long
book tour to places like New York, Los Angeles, Canada, En-
gland, France, Germany, and, my personal favorite, Puerto
Rico. Some of my most exciting experiences include taking
night cruises down the Seine River in Paris and walks across
the London Bridge and along the London Ghost Walk. I enjoyed being interviewed at the BBC Radio and World News
in London and by RTL TV in Cologne, Germany. It was a
thrill to watch my first Premier League Soccer game on a
crowded London rooftop pub, and I attended a very moving mass at Saint Rita Church in Paris (the saint of hopeless
causes). I even got to see the "Moulin Rouge" cabaret show
in Paris, and I saw my first Broadway play, *Kinky Boots,* in New
York City. And I relaxed on the beach and took horseback
rides through the beautiful mountainsides of Puerto Rico.

I've visited countries all across the world, speaking to people about my experiences. And wherever I went I tried to

soak up some of the language. After so many years of not being allowed to express my opinions or even speak at times, it's amazing to be able to talk to whoever I want and also to learn other languages.

Another high point was when Dr. Phil surprised me with a trip to Las Vegas to meet my favorite musician, Celine Dion. I had listened to Celine's music while I was locked up and held captive, and her songs helped me pull through some of my darkest hours.

In the past year I have done things I never even imagined possible. Yet one thing above all keeps me going: making sure that victims of abuse and mistreatment have something that I never had: a voice. I have spoken to and connected with so many people who are struggling with or recovering from abuse. And I will never be content until all of the victims' voices are heard. In fact, in May of 2014 I appeared live in Munich on the German program *Aktenzeichen XY . . . ungelöst* (*Case number XY . . . Unsolved*) with Rudi Cerne and four families who had lost children in the last year. I did my best to provide hope for the missing children's parents and families. Although I have already paved a long road, I don't want to stop leading the way in making sure that nobody ever feels alone and, most important, that nobody is forgotten.

As part of my healing process and to learn how to help others, last September I went as an inpatient to Milestone Onsite Recovery Center in Cumberland, Tennessee. There I worked with horses in their equine program, and through it I learned how to better communicate and interact with other people.

I still live in Cleveland, where I'm now enjoying my first real home. I spent hours decorating my house for Christmas, making up for all those years without a Christmas tree. And currently Lifetime is filming my life story in Cleveland. I was so excited to meet the actress who portrays me in the movie, Taryn Manning. At first I was a little reluctant to meet actor Raymond Cruz, who portrays Ariel Castro, but after seeing him off the set and having dinner together, Raymond and I have become friends.

A year ago I could only refer to Ariel Castro as "the dude" because I just couldn't bring myself to say his name. Now I can say it out loud, knowing that he cannot hurt me anymore. It's amazing what a year can do.

# Acknowledgments

None of this would have happened without Dr. Phil. He advocated for me and helped people connect with my story so that I could start a new life. I will be forever grateful.

I would like to thank my literary agents, Jan Miller and Lacy Lynch, for their commitment, help, and guidance with this book. Thanks also to the Dupree/Miller team: President Shannon Marven, Nena Madonia, Ivonne Ortega, and Nicki Miser for their hard work and support.

I would also like to thank Harvey Weinstein; Perseus Books Group CEO David Steinberger; Editorial Director Amanda Murray; Publishing Director Georgina Levitt; and Publicity Director Kathleen Schmidt. Many thanks to Leslie Wells for her thoughtful editing.

Appreciation goes to Michelle Burford for helping me with writing this book; to Christine Marra for production; to Deborah Feingold for the cover photos; and to Laura Hanifin for photo research.

Huge thanks to my friend Pastor Angel Arroyo, Jr., as well as to Charles Ramsay and Angel Cordero. Thanks to Commander Keith Sulzer and the Cleveland Police Department; to Anna Faraglia and the Cuyahoga County Prosecutor's Office; the staff at Metrohealth Hospital; contributors to the Cleveland Courage Fund; Tim Kolonick, Jennifer Meyers, and Lisa Miriello of the FBI; the Cleveland Chapter of the

Guardian Angels; and to Bob Friedrick. Also thanks to my friends at Happy Days Elderly Care. And a big thank-you to *Dr. Phil* Executive Producer Carla Pennington, and News Producers Erin Parker and Sarah Carden for all the help, and for being my friends.

Gina and Amanda, thanks for being my companions and best friends for the eleven years we were together. May God bless you for all the years you are free.

Finally, thanks to Abdoul Rahim AbdoulKarim, and to everyone at Giffen & Kaminski, LLC; and especially to my lawyer, Peggy Foley Jones, for her wise advice, and for always being there for me.